Minding the Gap

Appraising the promise and performance of regulatory reform in Australia

Minding the Gap

Appraising the promise and performance of regulatory reform in Australia

Peter Carroll, Rex Deighton-Smith,
Helen Silver and Chris Walker

ANU

THE AUSTRALIAN NATIONAL UNIVERSITY

E PRESS

Published by ANU E Press
The Australian National University
Canberra ACT 0200, Australia
Email: anuepress@anu.edu.au
This title is also available online at: http://epress.anu.edu.au/minding_gap_citation.html

National Library of Australia
Cataloguing-in-Publication entry

Title:	Minding the gap : appraising the promise and performance of regulatory reform in Australia / Peter Carroll ... [et al.].
ISBN:	9781921313158 (pbk.) 9781921313165 (web)
Series:	ANZSOG series
Notes:	Bibliography.
Subjects:	Business enterprises--Government policy--Australia. Business enterprises--Law and legislation--Australia. Deregulation--Australia. Trade regulation--Australia.

Other Authors/Contributors:
          Carroll, Peter.

Dewey Number: 346.94065

Cover design by John Butcher.

Funding for this monograph series has been provided by the Australia and New Zealand School of Government Research Program.

John Wanna, *Series Editor*

Professor John Wanna is the Sir John Bunting Chair of Public Administration at the Research School of Social Sciences at The Australian National University. He is the director of research for the Australian and New Zealand School of Government (ANZSOG). He is also a joint appointment with the Department of Politics and Public Policy at Griffith University and a principal researcher with two research centres: the Governance and Public Policy Research Centre and the nationally-funded Key Centre in Ethics, Law, Justice and Governance at Griffith University. Professor Wanna has produced around 17 books including two national text books on policy and public management. He has produced a number of research-based studies on budgeting and financial management including: *Budgetary Management and Control* (1990); *Managing Public Expenditure* (2000), *From Accounting to Accountability* (2001) and, most recently, *Controlling Public Expenditure* (2003). He has just completed a study of state level leadership covering all the state and territory leaders — entitled *Yes Premier: Labor leadership in Australia's states and territories* — and has edited a book on Westminster Legacies in Asia and the Pacific — *Westminster Legacies: Democracy and responsible government in Asia and the Pacific*. He was a chief investigator in a major Australian Research Council funded study of the Future of Governance in Australia (1999-2001) involving Griffith and the ANU. His research interests include Australian and comparative politics, public expenditure and budgeting, and government-business relations. He also writes on Australian politics in newspapers such as *The Australian*, *Courier-Mail* and *The Canberra Times* and has been a regular state political commentator on ABC radio and TV.

Table of Contents

Acknowledgements

The origins of this book lie in an invitation from Professor John Wanna to those responsible for the various streams of papers presented at the GOVNET Conference held at The Australian National University in December 2006, to submit sets of papers for consideration for publication as an ANU E Press monograph. It was felt that several of the papers presented in the 'Rethinking Regulation' stream, combined with a number of papers presented at other conferences and two specially commissioned chapters, provided valuable insights into the 'waves' of regulatory reform that Australia has experienced over the last 30 years, especially in regard to the successive attempts to improve the quality of the processes by which regulation is made and amended by government in conjunction with various stakeholders and interests. The result was this book, offering a wide range of views on several aspects of regulatory reform, prepared by authors who include academics, senior public servants and consultants. The book is an important contribution as it both describes and explains the reasons for many of the successes and failures of past reforms to regulation making processes at a time when Australia has commenced a third wave of reform, in the shape of the National Reform Agenda.

Contributors

Peter Carroll is a research professor in the Faculty of Business at the University of Tasmania, having been Dean of the Faculty from 2001–06. He was Professor and Head of the Department of Management at the University of Wollongong from 1999–2001 and, from 1997–99, Assistant Dean and Director of Graduate Studies in the Faculty of Business, Queensland University of Technology. He has research and consulting interests in the OECD, government regulation of business, policy transfer, innovation and policy analysis. His publications cover a variety of areas, including regulatory reform, innovation, regulatory compliance, international expositions, tourism and international business. He undertook several consultancies for the Queensland government as part of its major regulatory reform drive in the 1990s, focusing upon reviews of a number of acts, including the *Pharmacy* and *Optometry* acts, the *Tow Truck Act* and the *Radiation Safety Act*, as well as providing training in the process of regulatory review for public servants.

Rex Deighton-Smith is a director of a consulting company that provides specialist advice on policy and regulatory issues to governments, international organisations and the private sector. He previously worked on the Organisation for Economic Cooperation and Development's program on regulatory management and reform, where he contributed to several country reviews of regulatory processes. Rex is also a former director of the Victorian government's Office of Regulation Reform and has worked in policy areas in the Department of Treasury and Finance and the Department of Premier and Cabinet. He is an authority on regulatory impact assessment and the author of a number of publications on a range of regulatory policy issues.

Helen Silver is Secretary of the Department of Premier and Cabinet, Victoria, and was formerly the General Manager, Government Business — Business and Private Banking Australia at the National Australia Bank Limited. She was previously Deputy Secretary, Policy and Cabinet, of the Department of Premier and Cabinet and prior to that Helen held the position of Deputy Secretary, Economic and Financial Policy at the Victorian Department of Treasury and Finance. She has many years experience in senior management positions in the Victorian and Commonwealth public sectors, centred on the provision and management of high level policy advice and operational systems.

Chris Walker is a senior lecturer and the co-ordinator of the Master of Policy Studies in the School of Social Sciences and International Studies at the University of New South Wales. He has worked in various senior and middle level management and policy positions at the NSW Department of Health, the Roads and Traffic Authority and the Transport Safety and Reliability Regulator. Prior to joining the School, he was a member of the NSW Senior Executive Service working at the Cabinet Office. Chris has been on staff exchange with the Tokyo Metropolitan Government, Department of Health and worked on developing training material in public sector ethics for the Institute of Public Administration Australia. His research interests include intergovernmental relations, federalism, regulatory reform, public sector management and public sector reform. Of particular interest is the practice of separating policy from operations in government agencies and the consequences this presents for policy development and policy implementation.

Foreword

The GOVNET conference stream from which the chapters in this volume were drawn was titled 'Rethinking Regulation'. 'Rethinking' was what the *Regulation Taskforce* felt was called for if the causes, not just consequences, of the many poor regulations we observed were to be addressed. That, of course, is easier said than done, as some of the chapters in this volume attest.

The challenge facing aspiring reformers in this area reflects the reality, as one senior public servant put it, that 'no regulation is an orphan'. There are persistent demands on governments to 'do something' about issues of importance to particular groups. Such demands have both intensified and widened as our society has become more affluent and knowledgeable. That, of course, is democracy at work. It is to be expected. The resulting problems have more to do with how governments have responded to such claims through regulations, and how those regulations have been administered.

The Taskforce found not only an escalation in the stock of regulations, but also various deficiencies in their quality. Many regulations were found to be (among other things) overly prescriptive, poorly targeted, duplicative, mutually inconsistent, excessive in their coverage of firms and unduly onerous in the reporting and other obligations on the firms affected. Unintended consequences abounded.

How did this come about? Our report documents the reasons in clinical detail and more analysis can be found in this volume. But all the key ingredients can be illustrated in the following hypothetical scenario adapted from a speech I gave in 2006. Since no-one has subsequently contradicted me, I will assume that others too see it as a reasonable depiction of our regulatory processes at work.

A hypothetical regulation in the 'making'

A child is critically injured following a mishap with a skipping rope. On a slow news day, the story gets a run in one of the tabloids. A caller to the local radio talk show expresses alarm that 'these potentially lethal products' are still being sold. The compere, a high profile figure, expresses concern: 'Government inaction is putting our kids at risk!' The Minister is commanded to appear on his show. In the face of some torrid questioning and innuendo, she promises that her government will take firm action to eliminate the threat posed by skipping ropes.

Next day, the talk-back king pursues a new story (about bad language in public places). The Minister, however, feels obliged to instruct her department to take steps to put the government's new skipping rope policy into effect.

The department gets to it. Following a couple of conversations with the Minister's office, a proposal to ban skipping ropes is drafted for cabinet consideration.

However, a few days before cabinet is due to meet, someone recalls that any new regulation that may impose costs on business must have had a *Regulation Impact Statement* prepared, demonstrating the superiority of the preferred course of action. Panic stations!

An RIS justifying the ban is hurriedly put together by a junior departmental officer and submitted to the government's Regulation Unit, whose job it is to assist agencies and monitor their compliance with the government's RIS requirements. The Unit finds that the draft is inadequate on the key matters of demonstrating that any new government action is warranted and that a ban in any case would be the best option. [Consternation!]

A second draft, responding to some of the Unit's concerns, is quickly assembled and re-submitted. On a less significant matter, or with a less extreme regulatory option (and perhaps with more time) the revised RIS may have been helped over the line. As it is, the Unit is obliged to deny approval a second time.

Time is now up, however, and the submission proceeds to cabinet. A *Coordination Comment* from the Regulation Unit notes that the RIS was not adequate. The Minister (who has not read the RIS) concludes that the Unit is being obstructionist. Cabinet, aware of the origins of the new skipping rope policy — the little girl, the public outcry — agrees to the Minister's proposed ban. The Treasurer/Finance Minister has been briefed by his department about the adverse efficiency implications, but takes comfort from the fact that there are at least no budgetary implications. The Minister responsible for Industry knows that there are no local manufacturers of skipping ropes left — the last turned to importing when the tariff dropped below 15 per cent — so she too is comfortable.

I could conclude my hypothetical scenario there, as I think you get my drift. But this would omit the implementation phase, which as business groups told the Taskforce, can be as problematic as regulation-making itself in contributing to bad outcomes. So I'll go further. In this contrived example, cabinet could have decided that a 'black letter' ban on skipping ropes was going too far. (Maybe there was a small local manufacturer after all, perhaps in a country electorate, or maybe the already precarious relations with the main exporting country were seen as an issue). So, instead, the power to decide which skipping ropes are too dangerous for sale is delegated under a legislative amendment to the regulator.

Not being super-human, he (or she) is inclined to be cautious. He knows from painful experience that his agency will be lambasted publicly if any further mishaps occur, but receive no credit at all if skipping ropes are able to be used more liberally without mishap. So to be on the safe side, he issues a new subordinate regulation placing a range of conditions on the marketing and sale of all devices that could conceivably be used by children 'for the purpose, inter alia, of skipping or related activities'.

Things now start to get politically charged again, because the regulator has inadvertently affected some key Australian enterprises producing a variety of products, as well as many firms (and adult consumers) who use them. Moreover, firms producing related goods are obliged to incur labelling and other costs to stop their products from being used for skipping, as well as in convincing the regulator about their compliance. Complaints are made to government at different levels by the firms' industry associations.

Eventually a review of the regulation is conducted — possibly as part of a wider review of business 'red tape' — and the regulatory constraints are greatly eased and their product coverage reduced.

Moral of the story

While the subject of this little story was fanciful, a close variant could have been told based on any one of many actual examples at all levels of government, including some major regulatory initiatives in recent years. It therefore illustrates a number of failings in the way the legislative and other regulatory instruments of public policy have been developed. The key words are knee-jerk political responses, lack of analysis of costs and benefits, haphazard or limited consultation and, above all, a 'regulate first ask questions later' culture within parts of government; a culture that has been reinforced by a perception within the wider community itself that government action equals regulation.

All this needs to change if Australia is to meet its prospective social and environmental needs without compromising the economic growth that underpins living standards. For example, how we design the regulatory framework to achieve greenhouse emissions reductions looms as the critical determinant of the magnitude of the costs to our economy of achieving any particular targets.

A challenge for governments

Good regulation demands good processes for developing and administering it. The essential elements are not rocket science. They simply require clarity about the nature of a perceived policy problem and why intervention would help, and a detailed understanding of the pros and cons of different possible measures. To do this well, however, can be demanding. Among the key requisites are an ability to analyse the costs, benefits and risks associated with regulatory 'solutions', and to undertake effective consultation with those who bear these (not just those calling for action).

And because today's solutions may no longer be the right ones tomorrow, the periodic review of existing regulation is integral to achieving good outcomes over time.

There is nothing very novel in all this and, indeed, most governments, to varying degrees, have requirements in place, including regulation impact statements for significant regulatory proposals. What would be new would be their effective implementation and enforcement. This was what the Taskforce's recommendations were directed at, and many of its recommendations to entrench good process and practice have been adopted at the Commonwealth level. There have also been some steps forward within COAG, although the lowest common denominator appears to have prevailed thus far.

Ultimately, real progress will depend on the ability to change the 'regulate first' culture that is pervasive within government, and achieve a better appreciation within the wider community of the limits of regulation in dealing with society's complaints. I believe that procedural and institutional reforms will help on both fronts, but the critical ingredient for success will be political leadership.

Gary Banks
Chairman
Productivity Commission

Prologue

Peter Carroll

In a 2008 address to the Museum of American Finance entitled 'Lessons from Financial History', Niall Ferguson, the Laurence A. Tisch Professor of History at Harvard University and William Ziegler Professor at the Harvard Business School observed:

> Most regulations are improvised in the aftermath of a crisis. This is how regulations, generally, are produced. They almost immediately become inappropriate. So, regulators are always chasing the historical process. Like generals, they are always fighting the last war, never the next one.[1]

The quote is interesting and catchy — but almost totally incorrect as regards the assertion that regulations arise primarily in response to a crisis! The vast bulk of regulations are modifications to those that already exist. Occasionally, regulatory zeal is 'spurred on' because of a pressing, emergent issue and even, occasionally, a crisis, but not often. Life is more mundane than we like to think.

I do, however, agree with the latter part of the quote. Indeed, regulators, like generals, are often — if not always — fighting the last war. Regulation and regulatory responsiveness, rests on the art of catching up. This is not inconsistent with the 'policy arts' generally but, in the case of regulation, the goalposts — or the battleground (to preserve the analogy) — are constantly shifting.

Ferguson's address posits that financial markets, and the regulations that coalesce around them, exist in dynamic — almost organic systems. Regulators are almost always in a state of catch-up because the initial conditions prevailing at the time regulations are formulated are likely to have changed significantly by the time regulations have been promulgated.

Ferguson frames his remarks in the context of what he calls 'evolutionary economics' — the application of Darwinian theory to financial markets. Whatever one might think of such a construct, the metaphor of evolutionary niches has interesting applications to regulatory processes. Gaps in nature, after all, are prone to be filled. So too, gaps between regulation and the behaviours of the regulated will be filled — possibly with new behaviours requiring regulation! To the extent that the time lag between the articulation of a regulatory response and the gazettal of regulation gives rise to 'regulatory gaps', the regulatory process — like the environment within which it operates — needs to be dynamic and adaptive. The problem is, as the authors of this monograph observe, that regulatory processes are not as adaptive and dynamic as they should be.

In his 16 May 2008 speech to the Mortgage and Finance Association of Australia National Convention, the Minister for Superannuation and Corporate Law, Senator Nick Sherry, observed:

> … we are all operating in an increasingly complex and dynamic environment. And with this complexity comes risk. An optimal regulatory system will harness that risk, and allow us to achieve the right balance between protection, wealth and growth.[2]

Certainly, complexity and dynamism are givens in any policy environment as is the proposition that the management of complexity entails risk. The Minister's exhortation to 'harness risk' seems to suggest regulatory regimes and processes capable of acting in an almost entrepreneurial fashion to leverage community benefit from uncertainty in the environment. However, regulatory bodies exist also to exercise what might be broadly termed 'control functions' and, by nature, tend to be conservative both in their culture and operations. Managing risks and limiting the sometimes unintended impact of individual or corporate behaviour is, from this perspective, the essence of regulation. Institutional conservatism does not, of necessity, preclude creativity and foresight although experience tells us that the influence of stakeholders might result in governments accepting regulatory provisions that are sub-optimal, in effect, 'regulating' policy inventiveness.

That said, creativity and foresight are sorely required — particularly if the Rudd Government is serious about harmonising the regulatory regimes of the Commonwealth and State/Territory governments as part of its drive toward a less costly system of regulatory regimes. 'Getting the balance right', to employ one of the currently popular political catch-phrases, will be essential to the successful management of stakeholder interests. A recent survey commissioned by the Australian Securities and Investments Commission (ASIC) found — not surprisingly — that business thought the regulator should focus on principles rather than rules; collaboration rather than enforcement. Consumers, for their part, felt that regulators tread too softly and were not sufficiently robust in terms of enforcement or the application of sanctions.[3] Obviously, perceptions of and attitudes toward regulation will differ. Achieving 'balance' in ways that do not impose undue cost, unfairly transfer risk or compromise the public interest will never be easy.

The environment *is* complex, the risks *are* great and the rewards of success and the costs of failure will be enormous. The true measure of success will be how effectively we are able to close the gap between promise and performance. This book suggests that our abilities, based on observations of past performance, are limited.

ENDNOTES

[1] Professor Niall Ferguson, 'Lessons from financial history', broadcast 11 may 2008 on *Big Ideas*, ABC Radio National. The podcast of Professor Ferguson's address can be downloaded from: http://www.abc.net.au/rn/bigideas/stories/2008/2237927.htm

[2] Accessed 19 May 2008 at http://minscl.treasurer.gov.au/DisplayDocs.aspx?doc=speeches/2008/012.htm&pageID=005&min=njs&Year=&DocType=

[3] Emma Connors, 'Regulator gets mixed messages', *Australian Financial Review*, Monday 19 May 2008, page 5.

Chapter 1. Introduction

Peter Carroll

The aim of this monograph is to examine successive attempts by the Commonwealth government to improve the quality of the processes by which business regulation is made. Those attempts took place, for the most part, within three broader waves of microeconomic and regulatory reform that have occurred over the last 25 years. The first of these, which is not examined in this book, commenced in the early 1980s under the first of the Hawke ALP governments and was marked by major developments such as the floating of the dollar, substantial reform of financial market regulation (including de-regulation) and the rapid reduction of protective tariff barriers (Kelly 1992). The second wave of reform commenced during the Hawke and Keating Governments of the later 1980s and early 1990s and continued into the twenty-first century, under the auspices of the Council of Australian Governments (COAG) and the Howard Coalition governments. It was marked by two broad sets of reforms: one encompassed by the several hundred reviews of legislation and policy under the National Competition Policy (NCP), focusing on policy content; and the other related to reforms of the processes for making regulation, with the aim of ensuring that, in the future, new and modified regulation was not subject to the weaknesses that stimulated the NCP reviews. It is, as noted above, the 'process' reforms that constitute the primary focus on the book, as the NCP has been subject to considerable examination (with regard to NCP see, for example, Hollander 2006; Charles 2001; Deighton-Smith 2001; Butler 1996; Thomas 1996; Churchman 1996; Harman 1996). The third wave of reform commenced in 2006, often described as the National Reform Agenda, so it is somewhat premature to describe it as a major wave of reform, although that is its intent.

The remainder of this chapter is divided into three parts: the first and second parts provide brief overviews of the second and third waves of microeconomic reform in order to give a sense of perspective to the narrower concern with regulatory process that is the major concern of the book; the final section provides a brief description of the chapters of the book.

The second wave of reform: microeconomic reform in a federal state

The 1980s saw a growing concern in OECD countries for their poor economic performance since the early 1970s. It was a concern that found articulate and persuasive voice in the OECD's publication, 'Structural Adjustment and Economic Performance' (1987). The study argued that while the poor economic performance of member states certainly had been adversely influenced by the dramatic rise in oil prices during the 1970s, other major causes could be identified within domestic arenas, especially the failure of national governments to undertake those microeconomic reforms needed if their economies were to become more efficient. The study, in effect, endorsed and gave weight to those in Australia who had begun to push for a systematic program of microeconomic reform. Hence, it is not surprising, for example, that the Industry Assistance Commission (IAC), announced a two year inquiry strategy aimed at enabling it to identify impediments to microeconomic reform and improved national economic efficiency (IAC 1987: iv).

In Australia, in the more general context of economic reforms that had commenced in the 1970s and intensified in what became the first wave of reform under the Hawke Governments of the 1980s and early 1990s, the OECD concerns were reflected in a rising national concern for microeconomic reform (often described as structural adjustment or reform). As well as the more dramatic reforms associated with the floating of the Australian dollar, the rapid reduction in tariff barriers and the deregulation of the financial sector, there was evidence of a concern to ensure that, in future, the quality of regulation would be improved, with less negative economic impacts. This concern took institutional shape in the creation of a number of special purpose regulatory review units at both the state and federal levels, led by the Victorian Government. In 1986, for example, the Commonwealth's Business Regulation Review Unit (BRRU), was established. BRRU was given responsibility for reviewing existing and proposed Commonwealth legislation with regard to business (Wanna, Forster and Head 1991). This concern for the reform of regulatory processes was noted in Prime Minister Hawke's ALP Policy speech for the 1987 election and in his address to the Business Council of Australia, where he emphasised the need to re-shape economic institutions in order to meet the challenges of the 1990s (McAllister and Moore, 1991: 147; Hawke 1987: 1598).

It was a concern taken up by then Treasurer, Paul Keating in the same year and took on further significance with the transfer of the Industry Assistance Commission (IAC, now the Productivity Commission), to the Treasury portfolio. The significance lay in the fact that the Commission had begun to emphasise the inefficiencies that resulted from government regulation at both state and federal levels and the need for their reform and, with its transfer to the Treasury portfolio, it now had the ear of that powerful department and its very influential minister (see, for example, IAC 1986: 7, 8, 13-14, 18-19). The IAC made the need for regulatory reform the centrepiece of its 1988 annual report, in which it cited the OECD's 1987 study as evidence of the need for such reform (IAC 1988). In summary, it argued that the poor performance of the Australian economy was caused, in large part, by excessive protection and too much inappropriate regulation. In turn, protection and regulation were, for the most part, the responsibility of vested interests who 'sought preferment at the expense of the wider community', thereby hindering reform (IAC 1988: 4). It also stressed that 'progress in key areas is dependent on action by the States', drawing attention to the particular and frustrating difficulties of microeconomic reform in a federal state where much constitutional authority for business regulation lay in the hands of state governments (IAC 1988: iii, 15; 1989: 5-6). It emphasised what it saw as:

> ... a proliferation of ad hoc groups and permanent agencies advising on policy, each concerned with a particular part of the microeconomy and not always apparently bringing an economy-wide perspective to bear (IAC 1989).

The IAC's views bore fruit in August 1989 when Prime Minister Hawke announced the creation of a new body, the Industry Commission (IC), based on the IAC but including the BRRU and the Inter-State Commission, with closer coordination between the work of the new IC, the Bureau of Industry Economics and the Australian Bureau of Agricultural and Resource Economics — a coordination helped by the appointment of a senior Treasury official, Tony Cole, as chairman of the IC (IAC 1989: iii).

While greater administrative attention to regulatory reform was important, it needed substantial and public support from ministers at both the national and state levels if it was to be effective. This came in the shape of, first, a special series of Premiers' Conferences aimed at improving national efficiency and international competitiveness followed by the creation of the Council of Australia Governments (COAG). They signalled what soon came be to called a 'new federalism', designed in large part as an institutional mechanism to cope with the demands of widespread regulatory reform (see Carroll and Painter 1995; and Painter 1998 for more detailed elaborations). Within this promising political context three major developments resulted:

- one, the National Competition Policy (Productivity Commission 2005: xv for a fuller list of the NCP reforms);
- two, a parallel but separate series of reviews of regulations and related institutions, several leading to intergovernmental agreements and new, intergovernmental bodies such as the National Food Authority, National Grid Management Council and National Training Authority; and,
- three, the substantial strengthening of the Commonwealth's processes for making regulation, centred on the regulatory impact statement process (RIS).

While the first two were primarily concerned with reviewing existing policy and institutions, reforms to the process of making regulation aimed to ensure that future new or modified regulation would minimise regulatory burdens on the economy and businesses. Taken together, the three formed the core of what was now a widespread, national process of reform — one that continued into the new century (Fels 1995; Charles 1995; Harman 1996; Painter 1998; Hollander 2006).

There was considerable anticipation that, on coming to office in 1996, the first Howard Government would continue the Hawke-Keating reforms. Howard's 'neo-liberal' governments were not expected to disrupt the general thrust of the national process of reform set in train by the ALP at the state and national levels as, for the most part, Howard had been an ardent supporter of regulatory reform since his period as Treasurer in the last Fraser Coalition Government. More importantly, as Opposition Leader, Howard had criticised the Hawke and Keating Governments for not proceeding more rapidly with reform, albeit with differences in emphasis, rather than general intent (Quiggin 2004: 171). One of the more marked differences in emphasis in the early years of his first government, was in relation to the need to reduce the regulatory burden on small business, a sector he avidly courted in the 1996 election campaign. However, this proved an easy 'fit' in the ongoing program of regulatory reform. Greater differences did, of course, emerge in later Howard governments, notably in 2005, with the introduction of 'Work Choices', a dramatic change to the industrial relations system in Australia, aimed at freeing up labour markets and reducing the power of trade unions in what Howard proclaimed was one of the last major pieces of unfinished business in transforming the Australian economy (Howard 2005). Howard's efforts to further deregulate the labour market followed limited moves in this direction by previous Labor governments. The last Hawke Government and by the Keating Government in 1993 introduced measures to decentralise enterprise bargaining and Keating, in particular, had overseen a reduction in the power of the AIRC, the introduction of enterprise bargaining and had permitted registered collective agreements in the non-union sector.

The third wave of reform: 2006 and the future

The second wave of reform faded away somewhat unevenly and, with varying degrees of success, given the differing life spans of the three major developments, National Competition Policy (NCP) reform, regulatory reviews and process reform, based around the preparation of Regulatory Impact Statements (RIS). The reviews conducted as part of the NCP process are still ongoing as of the time of writing but for the most part are completed (Productivity Commission 2005). The various, separate, large scale, individual reviews were implemented at various times after 1996 and the RIS-focused reforms to the making of regulation were implemented by the Commonwealth in the 1996-8 period (Carroll 2006). Hence, the minds of decision-makers began to focus on the future: on the question of what to do next, with discussion focused in the Productivity Commission, COAG and, more generally, in the federal and state political executives, notably in the Victorian Government's 'Shared Future' project (Allen Consulting Group 2004; Banks 2004; Bracks 2005; COAG 2005; 2006a; 2006b; 2007).

In one sense, the answer to the question of what to do next had been partly determined by the results of the second wave of regulatory reform, notably by its less successful elements and those areas of regulation that it had not encompassed, suggesting that they now needed attention. Gary Banks, the Chair of the Productivity Commission, for example, in reviewing the NCP, concluded that it had yielded substantial benefits across the community but that the implementation process had not been perfect, that the public interest tests of existing regulation had not always been rigorously applied, that the independence of some reviews had been questionable and their conduct less than transparent and the outcomes of several key reviews rather problematic (Banks 2004). His view was reflected in the Productivity Commission's detailed assessment of the NCP Reforms a few months later (Productivity Commission 2005). Against this background, he suggested that:

- infrastructure reform must continue to be a high priority, especially in relation to energy, water and transport;
- not all anti-competitive regulation had been properly addressed — notably in relation to anti-dumping and cabotage regimes — as well as 'second round' reviews of wheat marketing, compulsory third party and workers' compensation insurance and the pharmacy sector;
- Australia's competition and regulatory architecture could be further improved, with an emphasis on improving regulatory processes, anti-competitive legislation, pricing regimes and consumer protection;
- coordinated national reform should extend beyond the current NCP to include health care and natural resource management but with a lower priority for aged care, education and training;
- health care and natural resource management were the highest priorities, particularly with regard to the overlapping responsibilities of the federal and state governments; and
- tax policy and labour market reforms should continue, building on what had been achieved (Banks 2004).

Banks' views were in several respects similar to those held by the Victorian Government of Premier Bracks. Some months earlier, in May 2004, the Allen Consulting Group had prepared a report for the Victorian Government that emphasised the need for a major new series of national, coordinated reforms in health and education, as part of the government's 'Shared Future', project (Allen Consulting Group 2004). These were endorsed by Premier Bracks and became the centrepiece of a new, national reform initiative he submitted to COAG, emphasising, in contrast to the earlier period of microeconomic reform, the need for reforms to human capital, constituting what he described as a 'third wave', of reform (Bracks 2005). The vision was described as one:

... of not only a strong economy, but also a healthy, skilled and motivated population where all enjoy the opportunity and incentive to be full and active participants in the life of the nation (Bracks 2005: 7).

It highlighted, in common with the views of Banks, the need for further development of economic competitiveness by undertaking regulatory reviews and building world-class infrastructure and the need for an improved health system but, in contrast, also the need to improve levels of educational and training achievement and the need to remove disincentives and barriers to labour force participation (Bracks 2005: 8). Interestingly, as with the OECD's 1987 report, the influence of the OECD on Australian policy debates again can be seen in Premier Bracks drawing upon an OECD report to support his case for a further wave of reform: a report that argued that Australia needed to achieve significant increases in productivity and participation if it was to rise to the never-ending challenge of international competition (Bracks 2005: 10, drawing upon OECD 2005).

In addition, Premier Bracks' vision differed somewhat from that of Banks with regard to the details of the institutional framework that would be necessary to achieve this 'third wave' of reform. Bracks' view was that, while COAG would retain primary responsibility for setting strategic directions, a National Reform Council should be established to guide the process. The Council might be assisted by bodies such as the Productivity Commission and it would appraise progress and make recommendations on funding flows according to a formula determined by COAG (Bracks 2005: 40-41). Also, it would be an independent body making recommendations to COAG on the funds needed for further work, albeit on the basis of a formula to be determined by COAG (Bracks 2005: 11, 40-47). Banks, in contrast, stressed that the successful implementation of the proposed reforms would require both leadership and inter-governmental cooperation on the basis of 'robust' arrangements that included well-articulated reform objectives and underlying principles, were based upon a rigorous analysis of options and provided means for the independent monitoring of progress (Banks 2005; Productivity Commission 2005). However, he had not provided any further detail, which came in the Productivity Commission's assessment of NCP reforms (2005, especially chapter 12).

The Commission, while supporting the general need for an effective institutional framework for the new wave of reforms, recommended that it be divided into two related parts: one, for reforms that were a continuation of those commenced under the NCP, the existing framework should continue to be used, focused on the National Competition Council and COAG; and two, for the reforms in health care and vocational education, 'stand-alone', sectoral programs should be developed. However, monitoring and reporting on reform progress and outcomes should be undertaken by a body or bodies independent of those responsible for policy development and implementation (Productivity Commission 2005: 380). In other words, progress and outcomes should be monitored by a politically neutral body, not any of the governments involved.

As might be expected, given a fair degree of policy consensus, the ALP state governments and the Coalition Government of John Howard had little difficulty in agreeing on the need for further reform if the Australian economy was to remain competitive. They had somewhat more difficulty in agreeing on exactly what should be done, notably, as regards institutional arrangements and funding. Compromise was reached in the form of a three-pronged reform agenda in 2006, with the announcement of a new 'National Reform Agenda', focusing on human capital, competition and, yet again, regulatory processes (COAG 2006a; 2006b). While it has excited surprisingly limited public and media attention to date, there is little doubt that the work it undertakes will become of increasing importance in the years ahead. This was made clear by the new Commonwealth government of Kevin Rudd that came to office in late 2007. It was committed to a continuing program of regulatory reform, including those put forward by the Taskforce on Regulation in 2006, arguing that the Howard governments had failed to continue the microeconomic reform process instigated by Labor governments in the 1980s and 1990s, with the result that the regulatory burden had grown and Australian productivity had fallen (Emerson 2007).

Rudd's critique of Howard seemed to imply that regulating reform was more rhetoric than reality; followed a pattern of 'punctuated equilibrium' followed by relative inertia; and proved difficult for governments to accomplish in the long term. We investigate these themes in the remainder of this book.

The structure of the book

As described above, this chapter has provided a brief introduction to the origins and development of the waves of regulatory reform that have characterised the work of Australian Commonwealth governments over the last 25 years. Chapter Two examines the development and performance of the Commonwealth government's Regulatory Impact Statement (RIS) system, designed to improve regulation-making processes in the somewhat ambitious hope that its output — regulation — would be of better quality and impose less cost in achieving the desired impacts on business. It argues that, in practice, the performance of RIS has been variable and less than was hoped — a performance explained by a number of factors, especially the fluctuating levels of ministerial and head of department/agency commitment to the system, a sometimes less than adequate integration of RIS with existing policy development processes and varying standards of analysis, particularly as regards the costing of regulatory proposals.

Chapter Three examines in more detail a neglected aspect of the Commonwealth's system for ensuring regulatory quality, the development and use of a system of regulatory performance indicators (RPIs) in the period 1998-2006. It provides a case study of the government's attempts to improve regulatory quality and performance, in line with the urgings of the OECD. Its conclusion is that the value and use of the RPIs was limited, although the experience gained should prove valuable in current attempts to improve existing systems of performance indicators (see Productivity Commission 2007).

Chapter Four, by ex-public servant turned academic, Chris Walker, argues that the processes of regulatory reform that have occurred since the early 1990s, with their emphasis on the need for regulatory uniformity and simplicity, have neglected the need to improve our capacity to manage complex regulatory and operational systems. Indeed, he suggests that one of the results of the reforms of the 1990s was the creation of more complex regulatory systems, which he illustrates with reference to railway systems and the role of the National Transport Commission. Rather than setting targeted programs of reform that strive for the holy grail of regulatory simplicity, he suggests that COAG should be seeking to transform arrangements within policy sectors so that agencies and stakeholders can better manage and respond to inevitable regulatory complexity.

Chapter Five is the first of three chapters that look forward, rather than back, in introducing the National Reform Agenda as proposed by the Victorian Government and endorsed by COAG. Its author, Helen Silver, played an important role in its development and promulgation. She argues the need for a further wave of reform at both state and federal level if Australia is to meet the major social and economic challenges it is facing, emphasising the need for cooperative reform within the COAG structure.

Chapter Six, by Peter Carroll, provides a critical assessment of the Commonwealth's Rethinking Regulation Program, based on the recommendations of the Banks taskforce and the government's response to its principal recommendations — a major plank in the third period of regulatory reform. Carroll's overall assessment is that while there is much in the report to be commended, the need is for greater commitment and support for existing systems for making and implementing business regulation rather than a fundamental rethinking of the system for making business regulation.

Chapter Seven, by consultant and ex-public servant Rex Deighton-Smith, notes that recent decades have seen a substantial move by regulators in Australia, as in many other OECD countries, to adopt performance-based and process-based regulation, in preference to traditional prescriptive regulation. This is a shift actively encouraged by regulatory reformers and the author argues that recent experience increasingly reveals a range of regulatory quality and regulatory governance concerns arising as a result of this trend. They include problems relating to transparency, public accountability and regulatory complexity and a set of recommendations are developed suggesting what might be done to improve performance.

References

Allen Consulting Group 2004, 'Governments Working Together: a Better Future for all Australians', a report prepared by the Group for the Victorian Premier as part of the Victorian Government's 'Shared Future', project, as at 30 May 2007, at http://www.dpc.vic.gov.au/CA256D800027B102/Lookup/Commonwealth_State_Relations/$file/PDF%20Final%20Version.pdf

Banks, G. 2004, 'NCP and beyond: an agenda for national reform', as at 30 May 2007, at http://www.pc.gov.au/speeches/cs20041206/index.html

Bracks, S. 2005, 'Governments Working Together - A Third Wave of National Reform - A New National Reform Initiative for COAG', based on Allen Consulting Group 2004, as at 30 May 2007, at http://www.dpc.vic.gov.au/CA256D800027B102/Lookup/A_Third_Wave_of_National_Reform/$file/A%20Third%20Wave%20of%20National%20Reform.pdf

Butler, G. 1996, 'National Competition policy: the downside', *Australian Journal of Public Administration*, v 55, no 2, June: pp. 104-105.

Carroll, P. and M. Painter (eds) 1995, *Microeconomic reform and federalism*, Federalism Research Centre, Australian National University, Canberra.

Carroll, P. 2006, 'Regulatory Impact Analysis: promise and reality', a paper presented to the ECPR/CRI Conference 'Frontiers of Regulation. Assessing Scholarly Debates and Policy Challenges', University of Bath, September 7-8 2006.

Charles, C. 1995, 'COAG and Competition Policy — A South Australian Perspective', chapter seven in Carroll and Painter (eds), *Microeconomic Reform and Federalism*, Federalism Research Centre, Australian National University, Canberra.

COAG 2005, *Review of National Competition Policy*, as at 30 May 2007, at http://www.coag.gov.au/meetings/030605/index.htm#com_policy

— 2006a, *A New National Reform Agenda*, as at 30 May 2007, at http://www.coag.gov.au/meetings/100206/index.htm

— 2006b, *National Reform Agenda (NRA): Human Capital, Competition and Regulatory Reform*, as at 30 May 2007, at http://www.coag.gov.au/meetings/140706/index.htm#reform

— 2007. *National Reform Agenda*, as at 30 May 2007, at http://www.coag.gov.au/meetings/130407/index.htm#mental

Charles, C. 2001, 'Reflections on National Competition Policy', *Australian Journal of Public Administration,* v. 60, no. 3, September, pp. 120-121.

Churchman, S. 1996, 'National competition policy: its evolution and implementation: a study in intergovernmental relations', *Australian Journal of Public Administration,* v 55, no 2, June, pp. 97-99.

Deighton-Smith, R. 2000, 'National Competition Policy: key lessons for policy-making and its implementation', *Australian Journal of Public Administration,* v 60, no 3, September, pp. 29-41.

Emerson, C, 2007. 'Lifting productivity growth by reducing business regulation', as at the

Australian Labor Party website at 9 January 2008, at http://www.alp.org.au/download/now/lifting_productivity_ growth_by_reducing_business_regulation_22apr07.pdf

Fels, A. 1995, 'Competition Policy, COAG and the Future', chapter six in Carroll and Painter (eds), '*Microeconomic Reform and Federalism*', Federalism Research Centre, Australian National University, Canberra.

Harman, E. 1996, 'The National Competition Policy: A Study of the Policy Process and Network', *Australian Journal of Political Science,* 31 (2): pp. 205-224.

Hawke, R. 1987, 'The Commonwealth Record', 11(36), 1598.

Hollander, R. 2006, 'National Competition Policy, Regulatory Reform and Australian Federalism', *Australian Journal of Public Administration',* 65 (2), pp. 33-47, June.

Howard, J. 2005, 'Statement on Workplace relations reform', House of Representatives, *Hansard,* p 39, 26 May.

IAC 1987, *Annual Report 1986-87',* AGPS, Canberra.

Kelly, P. 1992, *The End of Certainty. The Story of the 1980s,* Allen and Unwin, Sydney.

McAllister, I. and R. Moore 1991, *Party, Strategy and Change,* Longman Cheshire, Melbourne.

OECD 1987, *Structural Adjustment and Economic Performance,* OECD, Paris.

— 2005, *Economic Survey of Australia,* OECD, Paris.

Painter, M. 1998, *Collaborative Federalism- Economic Reform in Australia in the 1990s,* Cambridge University Press, Melbourne.

Productivity Commission 2005, *Review of National Competition Policy Reforms,* Report no. 33, Canberra.

— 2007, *Performance Benchmarking of Australian Business Regulation, Research Report,* Melbourne.

Quiggin, J. 2004, 'Economic Policy', chapter seven in Manne, R. (ed), *The Howard Years*, Black Inc. Agenda, Melbourne.

Thomas, C. 1996, 'Why national competition policy?', *Australian Journal of Public Administration*, v 55, no 2, June, pp. 100-103.

Wanna, J., J. Foster and B. Head 1991, in E. McCoy and B. Head (eds) *Deregulation or Better Regulation?* Macmillan.

Chapter 2. The Regulatory Impact System: Promise and performance

Peter Carroll

Introduction

The aim of this chapter is to provide an assessment of the performance of the Commonwealth government's Regulation Impact Statement (RIS) system, a system first introduced in 1986 but modified and strengthened in 1996 as part of a move to further improve the quality of new and modified regulation and, hopefully, minimise adverse impacts on business and economic performance. It argues that, while its proponents were keen to see its effective implementation in all departments and agencies — proposing that, as part of the broader process of regulatory reform, it would lead to an improved quality of regulation — actual practice showed that the performance of the RIS system was limited. It resulted in some improvements in the processes for making regulation, however, the quality of the resulting regulatory content and the analysis supporting that content improved little, if at all. It is further argued that this limited performance can be explained by a number of factors, especially the varying levels of ministerial and head of department/agency commitment to the system; a sometimes less than adequate integration of RIS with existing policy development processes; and, varying standards of regulatory analysis, particularly as regards cost/benefit assessments. The chapter is divided into three major sections: the first provides a brief, descriptive outline of the RIS system as modified in the mid-1990s; the second examines the performance of RIS from 1986-1997; the third examines its performance following reforms implemented during the period from 1998-2006 but prior to further modifications to the system introduced in late 2006.

The RIS system in the Australian Government

RIS is both a document and, most importantly, the documented result of a mandated process and approach to policy analysis intended to improve the quality of policy-making in the Australian Federal Government in relation to the regulation of business. At the heart of the process, as described by the Commonwealth's then Office of Regulatory Review (the ORR), were seven key elements that, when successfully completed, it was hoped would provide the decision-maker with the information needed to make an informed decision and better quality regulation. The seven key elements constituted a simple, rational, process-based model of policy-making familiar to all policy analysts, laying out the major tasks that were to be undertaken at each stage of the process, as follows:

- a description of the problem or issues which give rise to the need for action and broad goal of the proposed regulation;
- a specification of the desired objective(s);
- a description of the options (regulatory and/or non-regulatory), expressed as a regulatory form or type, that may constitute a viable means for achieving the desired objective(s);
- an assessment of the impact of each option on consumers, business, government and the community — including costs and benefits — noting particularly the impacts on competition, small business and trade;
- a consultation statement detailing who was consulted — with a summary of views from the main affected parties — or specific reasons why consultation was inappropriate;
- a recommended option, with an explanation of why it was selected and others were not; and
- a detailed strategy for the implementation and review of the preferred option (Office of Regulation Review 1998: A2).

The introduction of the RIS system predated the NCP reviews. In 1996-97 RIS was modified and became mandatory for all reviews of existing regulation, proposed new or amended regulation as well as proposed treaties involving regulation that would: directly affect business; have a significant indirect effect on business; or, restrict competition (Head and McCoy 1991; Office of Regulation Review 1998). The RIS system complemented the NCP reviews of existing regulation by focusing on future regulation. Its remit applied to all primary legislation, subordinate legislation and quasi-regulation — the latter referring to the wide range of rules or arrangements where governments influence businesses to comply but which do not form part of explicit government regulation (for example, industry codes of practice, guidance notes, industry-government agreements and accreditation schemes) (Office of Regulation Review 1998: A2-3).

The RIS did not apply to state, territory or local government in the Australian federal system, except insofar as any one or more of them were a party to a regulation developed on an intergovernmental basis within the Council of Australian Governments (COAG), although all bar one of the state and territory jurisdictions have RIS-type systems of their own. An RIS system is also applied by COAG, being largely identical with the federal RIS. In addition, RIS does not apply to tax regulation (although a modified type of RIS is used in this regard) and it is not applied in a number of relatively minor areas (Office of Regulation Review 1998: A4).

With regard to the relevant, mandated stages of RIS:

- departments, agencies and statutory authorities considering regulation that might impact on business were required to consult the ORR (now renamed the Office of Best Practice Regulation) at an early stage in the policy development process — the ORR had the authority to decide, in normal circumstances, whether or not an RIS was required;

- departments and agencies were required to consult with the ORR when developing terms of reference for reviews of existing legislation or regulations that impact on business;
- all RISs were to be developed in consultation with the ORR;
- draft RISs were to be sent to the ORR for comment and advice;
- the ORR was to advise departments and agencies whether or not a draft RIS complied with the government's requirements and, importantly, whether or not they contained an adequate level of analysis;
- the ORR was to receive all cabinet submissions proposing regulation or treaties and report to cabinet on both compliance with the RIS process and on whether or not the level of analysis was adequate;
- the Productivity Commission was to report annually on departmental and agency performance with regard to the completed RIS, both as to process and as to the quality of analysis provided in support of the proposed regulation;
- the Office of Small Business (the OSB), from 1999, also was required to publish a set of regulation performance indicators (RPIs) for departments and agencies — assisted by the ORR — and comment on regulation impacting on small business (Office of Regulation Review 1998:A10-14).

While the RIS process was and remains mandatory, the ORR's judgement as to the adequacy of an RIS process or analysis did not invalidate — or necessarily lead to the rejection of — a proposed regulation. That responsibility remained with the decision-maker involved, notably the Prime Minister and the Cabinet (Office of Regulation Review 1998: A12).

Regulatory performance and RIS: 1986-1997 a case of infant neglect?

RIS was introduced in 1986 as a new policy-making process coordinated by a new Business Regulation Review Unit (BRRU) (Head and McCoy 1991: 158). As noted in Head and McCoy, by the early 1990s, while it is difficult to assess the impact of the new system in any kind of detail, its impact, along with that of BRRU, seems to have been negligible (Head and McCoy 1991: 163). Indeed, insofar as the departments and agencies responsible for making and implementing regulation were concerned, there was no new system. Rather, at best, BRRU had encouraged departments and agencies to view the development of new or amended regulation with regard to business somewhat more critically, in line with the government's principle of the minimum of effective regulation (Industry Commission 1993: 272). In turn, BRRU provided advice to cabinet with regard to the regulations related to business that were submitted to it, advice that seems to have had little impact (Head and McCoy 1991: 163-4).

A number of factors account for RIS's lack of success at this stage. RIS was imposed upon departments and agencies by successive governments, eagerly supported by peak business associations and, increasingly, the government's own Productivity Commission. The departments were not enthusiastic about the imposition, with its implication that their existing policy development systems were inadequate. In addition, there was some feeling that the system had an ideological, rather than a regulation improvement purpose, aimed at freeing markets from regulatory control without convincing justification for the reform (Head and McCoy 1991). Also, RIS represented, at least in its earlier years, an increased workload and, if it was to be accommodated in the fashion desired by executive government, a degree of change to established processes and practices. Such organisational changes, welcome or not, take time to implement.

In 1988, a performance audit report of BRRU by the Commonwealth Auditor-General tended to confirm the above views but without reference to its ideological status, noting that it was not achieving its stated objective of comprehensively reviewing all targeted government regulation, or advising government on all new regulatory proposals, largely because of insufficient resources (BRRU had only six staff, plus a varying number of business executives seconded to it for short periods at this time), the lack of a comprehensive information base as to what regulations existed and the failure of some departments to provide the required RIS (Auditor General 1989). As a later publication noted of the period: 'ministers and regulatory departments/agencies routinely eschewed preparation of RISs' (Argy, Johnson 2003: 22). The Auditor-General's report and recommendations — perhaps combined with a desire to avoid business criticism of the lack of effectiveness of BRRU in progressing the review of business regulation — led to its 1990 transfer to an independent statutory authority, the Industry Commission, where it was given a new title, the Office of Regulation Review (Head and McCoy 1991:159).

Despite being brought under the authority of the Industry Commission, it soon became apparent that the ORR was continuing to have difficulty in achieving its objectives, as indicated by an external review conducted in 1993 (Industry Commission 1993b). The review noted that while the ORR had a useful role and had developed an effective framework for assessing the impact of regulation, there were several major constraints on its effectiveness, including deficiencies in the existing policy and procedural framework. As a result, it was:

- only able to comment on a small proportion of the total volume of new and amended business regulation introduced each year;
- consulted too late in the process to have a significant impact on the proposed regulation;

- constrained by the propensity of other government objectives to take priority over regulation review objectives; and
- devoting too many resources to its cabinet role (advice with regard to RISs that came to cabinet), relative to its other functions (Office of Regulation Review 1993: 271-2).

Thus, the review found that, in general, the ORR's formal responsibilities exceeded its capabilities and recommended that there be:

- a re-weighting of its work priorities to place greater emphasis on its educative and research role, with a more focused and selective approach to its cabinet role;
- measures introduced to increase awareness and understanding of regulation review policies within the bureaucracy; and
- measures to raise the public profile of the ORR and regulation review policy (Office of Regulation Review 1993: 272).

These conclusions indicated real limitations on the ability of the ORR to evaluate and comment on RISs and its ability to provide: (1) departments with advice aimed at improving regulation; or, (2) the cabinet with appropriate, timely advice as to the adequacy of submitted RIS in terms of either process or the quality and content of the proposed regulation. The reason was simple: the ORR did not have the resources to achieve these aims. In turn, this suggests that either successive governments had underestimated the resources necessary for the task, assuming that they were aware that this was the case, or they were not sufficiently concerned to increase resources to an appropriate level. In other words the necessary political and executive level commitment to, and support of, RIS, had not been forthcoming. It implied, also, that there had been little improvement in the quality of regulation-making in departments and agencies for — given that it was the ORR's role to promote such improvement and that it had not been able to do so to any great extent — then it was unlikely that they had improved their performance on pre-RIS times.

There is no systematic, quantitative empirical data on the performance of RIS for the 1986-96 period. However, some clues can be gained by looking at performance levels for the period 1996-97 — a period in which major changes to RIS were being put in place but were not yet fully operative and so were likely to have been similar to performance levels for the 1986-96 era. The data suggests that performance was very limited, with compliance with RIS being very low. Out of 121 Bills, for example, that required the preparation of a RIS for consideration by cabinet, departments provided the ORR with a RIS in only 13 cases (10.7%). This very low level of compliance with process at a time when greater political commitment to the reform of business regulation and RIS in particular, was being strongly expounded by the new government of Prime

Minister John Howard is surprising. As the ORR noted with regard to the pre-1996 period, 'there was little commitment to the process and a lack of any effective sanctions' (Office of Regulation Review 1997: 44).

In summary, much of the period from 1986 to 1997 had been a slow and somewhat painful period of birth and infancy for the RIS system, with widespread non-compliance with the process and little discernible impact on the quality and extent of new or amended regulation regarding business. A lack of political commitment and a lack of head of department and agency support resulted in policy development processes remaining largely unchanged with an under-resourced ORR often unable to discharge its advisory functions. However, at the end of this period, the political and public commitment of the new Howard Government together with the expanded coverage and authority given to RIS and other associated developments, suggested that the future might be more promising.

RIS performance 1998-2006: improving, but could do better?

In the period 1995-97 the RIS system was reformed as part of a broader set of reforms that commenced under the ALP government of Prime Minister Paul Keating but reached fruition in the first two years of the first Howard government. In summary, the major reforms were:

- the expansion of the ORR and an emphasis that RIS was mandatory;
- that RISs were to be tabled as part of the explanatory documents when proposals for legislative change were put before Parliament;
- that the Assistant Treasurer, although not a cabinet minister, be responsible for regulatory best practice, as a visible sign of a greater political commitment to regulatory reform;
- that the ORR was to report to cabinet on compliance with RIS requirements for specific regulatory proposals;
- the Productivity Commission was to report annually, in public reports, on overall departmental and agency compliance with RIS requirements, as regards both process and analytical quality, commencing in 1997–98 (Office of Regulation Review 1997; Productivity Commission 1998; Howard 1997); and
- the reforms were largely in line with the review and analyses produced for the first Howard government by the Productivity Commission and, especially, the *Bell Report*, that had investigated the impact of regulation on small business (Productivity Commission 1996; *Bell Report* 1996).

While the Productivity Commission and the ORR might have been happy with most of the general intent and recommendations of the *Bell Report* and the government's response to the report, the decision to establish a separate Office of Small Business (the OSB), with new regulatory review and reporting responsibilities, must have been of some concern. The OSB was to be consulted for all cabinet submissions that might have an impact on small business, including regulations of all types and to develop and report annually on a system of nine regulation performance indicators (RPIs). The departments and agencies would monitor and provide the OSB with the data related to their own performance, with the OSB reporting annually on their performance against the RPIs, with the first report to be made in 1999 (Productivity Commission 1999:12). RPIs were seen as an important adjunct to the RIS system, providing information on the effectiveness with which agencies were implementing regulation reform measures and enabling benchmarking of agency performance. In a somewhat clumsy arrangement, however, the ORR was to be responsible for collecting and monitoring agency performance in relation to three of the RPIs and for providing those details to the OSB (Productivity Commission 1999: 12). The situation was made even more awkward in 1998, for Prime Minister Howard committed his second government to the introduction of a system of annual regulatory plans for all departments and agencies in his 'A Small Business Agenda for the New Millennium', again to be reported on by the OSB, without the direct involvement of the ORR. The regulatory plans were to provide business and the community with timely access to information about past and planned changes to Commonwealth regulation, with the aim of making it easier for businesses to take part in the development of regulation.

In the first two years of the reformed RIS system (1996-97) compliance with RIS was, however, far lower than the average for the 1999-2006 period. As the Productivity Commission put it, these two years were a learning period for all concerned and it was expected that the level of compliance would improve (Productivity Commission 1999: xviii). It would have been more informative to have noted that there had been a learning period of at least 12 years, from 1986, not two years, with little systematic data on performance in the earlier period being collected. This little matter aside, the major reasons identified for the poor performance in these two years were, in summary: a lack of awareness of the requirements of the new system; varying degrees of understanding of and priority accorded to, the new system; a lack of resources for the ORR; and a slow process of cultural and organisation change resulting in a lack of integration of RIS into departmental policy processes (Productivity Commission 1998; and 1999).

In some cases, especially in regulatory agencies associated with COAG but also in some sections of major departments, communication of the new, reformed status and requirements of RIS simply had not percolated through to those with responsibility for making or amending regulation. Uncertainty about the coverage of RIS persisted even where communication had been effective, particularly in relation to subordinate legislation, quasi-regulation and treaties — to which it now applied (Productivity Commission 1998: xviii-xix). This lack of awareness and understanding applied particularly in COAG and the ORR noted that agencies associated with COAG claimed that they were not informed about, nor trained in, the new guidelines (Productivity Commission 1998: 70).

Rather embarrassingly for the new government, it was also apparent that several ministers' offices were not aware that the RIS requirements applied to them and, given the lack of awareness and understanding of what the reformed RIS now involved, it is not surprising that there were also examples of differences of opinion between the ORR staff and departmental staff as to how to interpret the RIS Guide (Productivity Commission 1998: xix). On a more positive note, for the relatively few RIS that were submitted in the 1996-97 period, the ORR felt that the level of analysis was adequate in 92% of cases (Office of Regulation Review 1997: 44).

What then, was the performance of this new, reformed RIS after the initial learning period? In terms of volume, as indicated in Table 2.1, in the period from 1999-2000 to 2004-05, a total of 11,545 Bills and Disallowable instruments were introduced, with the ORR receiving 4,832 new RIS queries with regard to this total, of which it advised that 1,085 (9.4%), required an RIS. The relatively small proportion of Bills and instruments subject to RIS was because most of the latter involved minor amendments to existing regulation that did not require the preparation of an RIS (Productivity Commission 2005: 79).

Table 2.1 Australian Government regulatory and RIS activities, 1999-2000

	1999-2000	2000-01	2001-02	2002-03	2003-04	2004-05
Total number of regulations introduced	1991	1607	1918	1789	1688	2552
Queries for which the ORR advised an RIS was required	266	171	175	132	174	167
% RIS of total no. of regulations	13.3	10.6	9.1	7.3	10.3	6.5

(See Productivity Commission 2005: 78, for further details)

In aggregate, the extent to which the RISs submitted by departments and agencies were regarded as *adequate*, using the measures developed by the ORR, is indicated in Table 2.2, below, for RIS at both the decision-making stage of the regulation-making process and the Parliamentary tabling stage (see Productivity Commission 2000, chapter three, for a description of how the measure is calculated). On average, 84% of the RISs at the decision-making stage were regarded as adequate, rising to 92% for the parliamentary tabling stage — the higher rate for the latter being, perhaps, a function of the greater risk of causing embarrassment for the minister, the government and the department if an inadequate RIS was provided for parliamentary and public scrutiny. The lower rate of adequacy for RIS developed at the decision-making stage was of concern, as it suggested that at least 16% of decisions on proposed new, or amended regulation, were made on the basis of inadequate information, at least as judged by the ORR.

However, what also becomes evident is that the overall levels of RIS performance indicated in Table 2.2 for the crucial, decision-making stage, concealed marked variations in regulation performance. In particular, the levels of compliance achieved for more *significant*, new or modified regulation was substantially lower than the overall average for all regulation, even though it might be expected that departments would be most careful in the adequacy of their analysis for more significant regulation. The average level of compliance for the 2000-05 period for more significant regulation, for example, was only 68%, compared to 87% for less significant regulation. It also fluctuated considerably from year to year, ranging from a low of 46% for more significant regulation in 2002-03, after some four years of experience with the new system, to a high of 94% a year later. There was less but still considerable fluctuation for less significant regulation, from a high of 92% in 2003-04.

Table 2.2 RIS compliance, 1999-2000 to 2004-05

Decision-making stage	1999-2000	2000-01	2001-02	2002-03	2003-04	2004-05
No. of RIS required	169	129	128	113	105	68
No. of RIS judged adequate	207	157	145	139	114	85
%	82	82	88	81	92	80
Parlt. tabling stage						
No. of RIS required	163	118	116	113	82	59
No. of RIS judged adequate	179	133	123	119	86	66
%	91	89	94	95	95	89

(See Productivity Commission 2005: 15, for further details)

There is a similar variation in performance when RIS are broken down into primary legislation (Bills), legislative instruments (largely subordinate legislation), non-legislative instruments, quasi-regulation (largely codes of conduct and target requirements) and RIS prepared for treaties. With regard to primary legislation the adequacy of performance fell from 80% in 1999-2000, to 76% in 2004-05, suggesting that RIS performance was not improving, even if it was not getting substantially worse, a disappointing result after eight years of operation for the new RIS system. The RIS performance for treaties, while involving only small numbers per annum and those treaties for which negotiations had commenced before the new RIS system came into effect, was very poor. As might be expected, the variation in aggregate RIS performance is mirrored in variation by department and agency. While the total number of RIS for each of the 19 departments and agencies whose proposals required an RIS is relatively small, only 10 departments and agencies were fully compliant at the decision-making stage in 2004-05 — a sharp drop from 2003-04. Nine departments or agencies were not compliant in whole or in part and the nine failed to develop, in total, some 14 RIS, with three of those that they did prepare having an inadequate level of analysis (Productivity Commission 2005: 31).

With regard to RISs prepared for COAG, performance was poorer, with the average for the period being 76%, nearly 10% lower than that for the decision-making stage for non-COAG RIS (Productivity Commission 2005: 66). There was also considerable variance in the performance by Ministerial Council and National Standard Setting Bodies within COAG (Productivity Commission 2005: 66-7). Despite this variable performance there was a substantial average increase in *process* performance over the whole of the period 1996-2006 but it was an increase that had largely peaked by the beginning of the 2000s, following the rapid increase in 1998-2000 and the quality of *content* of RISs improved more slowly.

What factors help explain this variable and sometimes disappointing RIS performance, even if the very poor performance in the learning period, 1996-98, is not included? In drawing upon the sources available four broad factors seem to have been of most importance. They are:

- RIS system design factors and poor communication of expectations;
- varying degrees of failure to integrate RIS into traditional departmental and agency policy development processes;
- limitations in analytical expertise; and
- varying levels of political commitment and support (Banks 2006a: chapter seven).

Deficiencies in the design of the RIS system itself have become apparent over time and were highlighted in the recent *Banks Report*, which found, in assessing both RIS and departmental policy development processes, that the requirements for good regulatory process had generally not been well discharged, agreeing with business groups that this had been a major contributor to the problems identified with specific regulations (Banks 2006a: v). One of the major limitations was the relative lack of initial emphasis in the RIS process on the need for at least adequate consultation with business in designing regulations, leading, it could be argued, to poorer quality regulation. A survey undertaken by the Australian Public Service Commission, for example, found that only 25% of regulatory agencies had engaged with the public when developing regulations, a surprisingly low proportion (Australian Public Service Commission 2005: 56). While it does not necessarily follow that limited or no consultation will result in poorer quality regulatory proposals, it is certainly possible and, where they do occur, will tend to alienate the businesses upon which regulation impacts. There is, of course, something of a dilemma with regard to increased consultation, for, if the RIS and the ORR called, as they did, for greater and more effective consultation, then it might also increase the danger of regulatory 'capture', by business interests.

A second limitation was the ineffectiveness of the system of regulatory performance indicators (RPI) introduced in 1998 and managed by the Office of

Small Business. The RPI were introduced in order to provide information for decision-makers as to departmental, process-based performance with regard to business regulation (Carroll 2007). However, in practice they had little or no impact on departments, with few departments or agencies using them — at least not explicitly or in published sources — as a means of identifying the causes of poor performance or for improving on existing performance. In this regard it is interesting to note that the recent *Banks Report* on the performance of the existing RIS system made no specific mention, positive or negative, of the existing system of RPI. Similarly, while the government agreed to all of the recommendations of the *Banks Report* with regard to the need for better performance indicators it made no specific reference to the existing system of RPI, either positive or negative. The failure, in both cases, to provide an assessment of the RPI implies that they were regarded as relatively ineffective, or not well known, or both — a view supported by most of those interviewed by the author in a range of government departments and agencies. Indeed, it proved difficult to locate persons within departments who were aware of the existence of RPI. Those that were aware indicated, for the most part, that the RPI had been of restricted value and were rarely used by departments in considering their performance. Yet, the information was available, if not used, suggesting that there was a considerable reluctance by ministers and senior officials in line departments and the Cabinet Office to take firm action to improve performance.

A frequently noted cause of poor RIS performance by the Productivity Commission, in both its annual reviews of regulation and by its chair and other senior staff, was a continuing failure on the part of some departments and agencies to fully integrate the RIS system with their established policy development processes (see, for example, Productivity Commission 2005: xx, 25). The result, too often, was that staff tended to regard RIS as merely an 'add on' to established departmental procedures, producing the necessary RIS documentation too late in the decision-making process to have any influence, after the proposed regulatory approach had already been determined. There were a number of reasons for this lack of integration:

- a continuing lack of belief in the RIS system and its value by at least some ministers and senior public servants, resulting in a less than full commitment to support its integration and a lack of effort and enthusiasm by those responsible for undertaking RIS within departments; and
- the continuing lack of experience in the application of RIS by public servants.

In the case of any one department only a limited number of RIS are required per annum and those that are conducted are allocated, very often, to different staff in different divisions within the same department, often to those with responsibility for the regulatory area in question. Hence, unless the department has only the one centrally-located policy development unit with staff serving with the unit for several years (which is normally not the case) then it is unlikely that any one individual or group of individuals gains expertise in with RIS, even over a period of years, a phenomenon noted by ORR staff.

One of the key causes of poor quality regulatory proposals has been varying and often inadequate levels of analysis by departments and agencies, especially of the costs and benefits of the regulatory options identified in their RIS. This has been of continuing concern to the ORR and the Productivity Commission, with, for example, recent examples of inadequate analysis including a department not clearly identifying the problem the proposed regulation was supposed to address, another not containing a summary of views received from stakeholders and the community, nor any discussion of how these views had been considered and another not providing any quantification of regulatory compliance costs (Productivity Commission 2005: 26). Where RIS were prepared but failed the ORR adequacy test, an inadequate analysis of costs, benefits and impacts on business, small and large, was typically the case (Productivity Commission 2005: 26). Productivity Commission concerns about poor levels of analysis led its chair, Gary Banks, to assert that 10% of tabled RIS did not even consider compliance costs and only 20% made an attempt at quantifying them (Banks 2005: 10). Similarly, a study of Victorian State government RIS and a small sample of COAG RIS in 2001 found that those conducted on behalf of the state government were clearly superior on all 10 of the criteria used in the study to those conducted for COAG (Deighton-Smith 2006).

As noted above, political support for RIS varied in extent and intensity over time. The primary reason for the variation is not hard to find, occurring, in particular, where ministers are faced, for example, with an RIS assessment that judges their new or modified regulatory proposal as not adequate. In such situations they face a quasi-conflict of interest situation: on the one hand committed under the doctrine of collective cabinet responsibility to support cabinet's formal support for RIS and the ORR's assessments of adequacy but, on the other hand, faced with a failed regulatory proposal if the RIS evaluation is negative. Moreover, the staff of ministerial offices, the heads of departments and senior public servants are well aware of this situation. Whatever their personal feelings on the matter, it would be a very brave person who resisted the wishes of a minister by advising that a favoured regulation was not to be recommended and pursued, following an averse RIS assessment from the ORR.

Similarly, when judging an RIS to be inadequate, it is difficult — but not impossible — for the ORR and Productivity Commission staff, even at the most senior levels, to gain the agreement of the department involved of the need to improve the RIS in question. It is even more difficult to persuade them to amend or withdraw a RIS, especially where it has been presented to the ORR at the very last minute and cabinet awaits its submission (Productivity Commission 2005:

82). In recognising this situation, it is rare for the ORR to pursue the matter to the ministerial level. Instead, its staff elect to work more informally with departmental and ministerial office staff in an attempt to amend proposed regulations identified as less than adequate. In this they have had some success. In 2004-05, for example, the ORR was successful in 10 of 71 RIS cases, in persuading departments to modify the preferred regulatory option contained in their RIS (Productivity Commission 2005: 83). However, as RIS have the status of cabinet submissions they are not, at least at the final, submission stage, released for more public scrutiny, so little or no public pressure can be brought to bear by this means on RIS that the ORR regard as inadequate (Productivity Commission 2005: 81).

Conclusion

In essence, the RIS was and continues to be a major attempt to improve the quality of regulation with regard to business. As noted above, in practice its performance has been variable and limited. Departments and agencies have improved, if to varying extents, their performance with regard to meeting RIS *process* requirements but they have been less successful with regard to improving the *content* of new and amended regulation.

Finally, it has to be remembered that any system for policy-making in a democracy, inevitably and continuously, will be subject to competing political forces, from those desiring change for the benefits they hope it will bring, to those who resist change, for fear the benefits that they currently receive will diminish or be eliminated. Policy-making — whether or not it is referred to as regulation-making — is an intensely political process and occurs in an arena in which regulation-making is determined as much by the relative power of the participants as by process and the quality of regulatory content. Efforts to promote a greater degree of rationality, such as RIS, are to be welcomed for any improvements in content and process performance they might bring but they are not immune from the exercise of power in the policy process. This is the central problem faced by RIS and its adherents. It is the reason that popularly elected ministers will always vary in their degree of support for such a system, for they are players in that process, acutely sensitive to its demands and constraints. If they are not, they do not remain as ministers for any length of time.

References

Australian Government 2006, *Rethinking Regulation: Report of the Taskforce on Reducing Regulatory Burdens on Business Interim Response*, as at 28 June 2006, at http://www.pm.gov.au/news/media_releases/media_Release1869.html

AIG 2004, *Compliance Costs Time and Money*, Australian Industry Group, as at 12 June, 2006, at http://www.aigroup.asn.au/aigroup/pdf/economics/surveys_and_reports/economics_reports_compliance_Oct4.pdf

Argy, F. And M. Johnson 2003, *Mechanisms for improving the Quality of Regulations: Australia in an international context*, Productivity Commission Staff Working Chapter, July.

Auditor-General 1989, *Reports on audits to 31 December 1988*, Australian National Audit Office, AGPS.

Banks, G. 2001, *Challenges for Australia in Regulatory Reform*, as at 14 June 2006, http://www.pc.gov.au/speeches/cs20010710/index.html

— 2003a, *Reducing the business costs of regulation*, March, Productivity Commission, as at 12 June 2006, at http://www.pc.gov.au/speeches/cs20030320/index.html

— 2003b, *The good, the bad and the ugly: economic perspectives on regulation in Australia*, 2 October, Productivity Commission, as at 12 June 2006, at http://www.pc.gov.au/speeches/cs20031002/index.html

— 2004, *NCP and beyond: an agenda for national reform*, 6 December, Productivity Commission, as at 12 June 2006, at http://www.pc.gov.au/speeches/cs20041206/index.html

— 2005, *Regulation-making in Australia: is it broke? How do we fix it?*, 7 July, Productivity Commission, as at 12 June, 2006, at http://www.pc.gov.au/speeches/cs20050707/index.html

— 2006a, *Rethinking Regulation*, January, as at 12 June 2006, at http://www.regulationtaskforce.gov.au/index.html

— 2006b, *Reducing the Regulatory Burden: the way forward*, 17 May, Productivity Commission, as at 12 June, 2006, at http://www.pc.gov.au/speeches/cs20060517/index.htm

BCA 2005a, *Locking in or Losing Prosperity — Australia's Choice*, Business Council of Australia, as at 12 June 2006, at http://www.bca.com.au/content.asp?newsID=99077

BCA 2005b, *Business Regulation Action Plan For Future Prosperity*, Business Council of Australia, as at 28 June 2006, at http://www.bca.com.au/content.asp?newsID=99099

Bell, C. 1996, *Time for Business*, the Report of the Small Business Deregulation Task Force, as at 11 June 2006, at http://www.daf.gov.au/reports/time_for_business.pdf

Brennan, G. 2004, 'The Political Economy of Regulation: A Prolegomenon' in G. Eusepi and F. Schneider (eds) 2004, *Changing Institutions in the European*

Union: A Public Choice Perspective, Edward Elgar Publishing, Cheltenham, pp. 72-94.

Carroll, P. 2007, 'Measuring performance in the public sector: the value of regulatory performance indicators', IRSPM Conference, 2-4 April, University of Potsdam.

Deighton-Smith, R. 2006, personal communication with the author.

Head, B. and E. McCoy (eds) 1991, *Deregulation or Better Regulation?*, Macmillan, South Melbourne.

Howard, J. 1997, *More Time for Business*, statement by Prime Minister Howard, as at 11 June 2006, at http://www.industry.gov.au/content/itrinternet/cmscontent.cfm?ObjectID=25D8598E-CFE8-47EA-BC45A29D63948869

Industry Commission 1993a, *Developments in Regulation and its Review*, 1992/3', Industry Commission, AGPS, as at 12 June 2006, at http://www.pc.gov.au/orr/reports/annrpt/reglnrev9293/index.html

— 1993b, Review of the Office of Regulation Review, Industry Commission, AGPS.

— 1994, *Annual Report 1993/4*, Industry Commission, AGPS.

— 1995, *Annual Report 1994/5*, Industry Commission, AGPS.

— 1996, *Annual Report 1995/6*, Industry Commission, AGPS.

— 1997, *Regulation and its Review: 1996-97*, Industry Commission, AGPS.

OECD 2001, Businesses' Views on Red Tape: Administrative and Regulatory Burdens on Small and Medium-Sized Enterprises, OECD, Paris.

Office of Regulation Review 1993. *Regulation and its Review, 1992-1993'*, Industry Commission, Canberra.

Office of Regulation Review 1997, *Regulation and its Review, 1996-1997*, Industry Commission, Canberra.

Office of Regulation Review 1998, *A Guide to Regulation* (second edition).

Productivity Commission 1996, *Stock take of progress in microeconomic reform*, June, AGPS, Canberra.

Productivity Commission 1998, *Regulation and its Review 1997-98*, AusInfo, Canberra.

Productivity Commission 1999, *Regulation and its Review 1998-999*, AusInfo, Canberra.

Productivity Commission 2000, *Regulation and its Review 1999-2000,* AusInfo, Canberra.

Productivity Commission 2001, *Regulation and its Review 2000-01*, AusInfo, Canberra.

Productivity Commission 2002, *Regulation and its Review 2001-02*, Annual Report Series, Productivity Commission, Canberra.

Productivity Commission 2003, *Regulation and its Review 2002-03*, Annual Report Series, Productivity Commission, Canberra.

Productivity Commission 2004, *Regulation and its Review 2003-04*, Annual Report Series, Productivity Commission, Canberra.

Productivity Commission 2005, *Regulation and its Review 2004-05*, Annual Report Series, Productivity Commission, Canberra.

Self, P. 1977, Econocrats and the Policy Process: the politics and philosophy of cost-benefit analysis, Westview Press.

Chapter 3. Measuring Regulatory Performance

Peter Carroll

Introduction

The aim of this chapter is to describe and assess the development and use of the system of regulatory performance indicators (RPI) by the Commonwealth Government in the period 1998-2006. The RPI were designed to provide decision-makers with standardised, system-wide data on the largely RIS-related processes by which departments developed regulation with regard to business. As such, they were early examples of a more general, international move to improve regulatory quality and performance, in line with the urgings of the OECD (see, for example, OECD 2004a; and 2004b).

The chapter concludes that the value and use of the RPI was limited, although the experience gained should prove valuable in current attempts to improve existing systems of performance indicators. The chapter is divided into three parts and a conclusion. The first part describes the context in which the system of RPIs was developed. The second identifies and discusses some of the major design limitations of the final set of nine RPI that were developed. The third assesses the performance of departments as indicated by the RPI, including an assessment of the value of the RPI themselves.

Context: the RIS, the RPI and the nature of the RPI challenge

The origins of the existing system of RPI in the Australian national government can be found in two sources: firstly, in the more general concern to ensure successful regulatory reform by improving and making more rigorous the processes for formulating new or modified regulation; and secondly, in the greater emphasis placed by Prime Minister Howard on the need to reduce the regulatory burden on small business, a theme he stressed in the 1996 election campaign (Howard 1997: iii). On gaining office a National Small Business Summit was called, meeting in June, 2006. The summit endorsed a 'Charter of Principles', in relation to the government regulation of business, endorsed by all levels of government, with the tenth principle asserting that Australian governments should develop a system of performance indicators to measure the efficiency of their regulatory regimes (SBDTF 1996: 150).

A major outcome of the recommendations of the National Summit was the establishment in 1996 of the Small Business Development Task Force (SBDTF) to review the 'compliance and paper burden imposed on small business'. The Task Force reported in November 1996 (SBDTF 1996: vii). The report referred to RPI in three contexts: one, in relation to the need to establish a set of performance indicators that would enable both the government and small business to track Government's performance in implementing the report's recommendations; two, in relation to the need for the development of a set of benchmarked, nationally comparable performance indicators for regulation that would enable more effective management of the growing regulatory burden by providing accurate information; and three, related to the second, the need for more detailed, varying sets of indicators at the departmental and agency level (SBDTF 1996: 131-34, 148). The report recommended 10 performance indicators relating to: transparency; accessibility; appropriateness; predictability; flexibility; lower cost to business; administrative efficiency; fewer and simpler forms; better instructions; reduction in perceived burden; and cultural change (SBDTF 1996: 131).

The Government's response to the report was generally positive. In particular, it agreed to one recommendation (number 62) that a national set of performance indicators and benchmarking strategy should be developed (Howard 1997: vii, 81-82). It noted that a meeting of small business ministers and the Australian Local Government Association already had agreed that the adoption of appropriate performance indicators was crucial and that a working group of officials would develop policy options for implementing comparable performance indicators for consideration at the next Small Business Summit (Howard 1997: 82). In addition, it noted that the Commonwealth Government had stressed the need for all departments and agencies to continue to develop 'meaningful and measurable' performance indicators capable of demonstrating the following properties:

- meeting essential regulatory objectives without unduly restricting business;
- regulatory decision-making processes are transparent and lead to fair outcomes;
- consultations with industry and the public have been implemented that are ongoing, accessible and responsive;
- information about the content of, and compliance with regulation is widely available to, and understood by small business;
- new or revised regulation confers a net benefit on the community; and
- a predictable regulatory environment is created so business can make decisions with some certainty (Howard 1997: 82).

While expressed rather differently, the latter six indicators covered all of the areas recommended in the SBDF Report with two exceptions: the indicator intended to measure the achievement of a 'lower cost to business'; and, the indicator for administrative efficiency. The Government noted only that there was a need for an indicator capable of demonstrating that new or revised regulation would confer 'a net benefit on the community' without any mention of reducing costs to business, although this could reasonably be inferred, given the context of the Prime Minister's message (Howard 1997: 82). It made no mention of an indicator related to administrative efficiency and provided no explanation as to why indicators for these two areas had been omitted.

While the members of the SBDF and their supporters inside and outside government might well have been satisfied with their success in gaining acceptance for the bulk of their recommendations there were, with the exception of the 'lower cost' and administrative efficiency indicators, limitations and significant challenges in what they had proposed and what the government endorsed. Four stand out as of particular importance. The first, as noted above, was the failure to specify an indicator in relation to business costs, although any calculation of the net benefit to the community of regulation (see the fifth dot point above), if sufficiently rigorous, would necessitate the calculation of business costs as part of the calculation.

The second limitation was the neglect of any recommendations for indicators that would enable departments, agencies and, ultimately, cabinet, to measure the performance of existing business regulation in actually achieving its specified objectives. This was in marked contrast to its very clear view that the existing systems and processes for indicating the quality of *new* and *modified* regulation needed improvement. The neglect may have been deliberate — an implicit acknowledgement of the difficulties of such a task — but it was a limitation that left the government (and, importantly, the working party of officials charged with developing policy options as well as federal departments and agencies) free from the explicit requirement to consider and recommend how such a system might be developed and implemented. This was unfortunate for, in a parallel development, departments at this time were increasingly being required to introduce systems of output and outcome plans and budgets with associated performance indicators, within which any desired RPI could have been embedded (Department of Finance and Administration 1999; and 2007; Department of the Prime Minister and Cabinet 2007).

The third limitation was the failure of the government, as noted above, to specify indicators of administrative efficiency in relation to the implementation of regulations. This may have been because it was realised that several systems were already in place — or being put in place — and that these were regarded as sufficiently informative. Examples included the annual parliamentary reviews of departmental expenditures, the performance audits of the Australian National Audit Office and departmental annual reports. The latter contained the departments' report of their performance against their outputs and outcomes, using performance indicators specified in the PBS — but not the desired RPI —

although there was nothing to prevent such indicators being developed and used by departments. It is interesting that they have not included RPI because, in conjunction with the PBS performance reports, they would have provided a fuller picture of regulatory performance.

The fourth limitation was the SBDF's failure to recommend that responsibility for RPI at the 'broad policy level' be established under the control of the existing Office of Regulation Review (the ORR). As the ORR was a unit in the influential Productivity Commission — and located, therefore, within the broader Department of the Treasury portfolio — this might have provided it with an important source of power in relation to the design, implementation and use of RPI.

In summary, while the move to develop a set of RPI that would enable the comparison of regulatory performance across departments and agencies was a marked step forward in the effort to improve regulatory quality, the relative lack of focus on: the development of indicators for specific businesses compliance costs; the achievement of regulatory objectives; administrative efficiency in implementing regulations; and an appropriate organisational location, suggested that any resulting RPI system would be less than optimal.

Design limitations of the RPI system: regulatory coverage, integration and type of RPI

In the course of 1997-98 two Government commissioned studies of performance indicators were undertaken. The first was by the government's then Industry Commission (now the Productivity Commission). Because the study was not established to provide information and recommendations for the government in relation to the recommendations of the *Bell Report*, its terms of reference confined it to the examination of national and comparative performance indicators for local government. The origins of the study, in fact, predated the *Bell Report* and it did not include indicators for State and Territory governments except insofar as the latter used indicators with regard to local government performance. The report's conclusion was that a consistent, national approach to performance measurement for local government was not 'warranted', at that time (Industry Commission 1997a: vii). It did, however, note that further discussion might, in time, lead to 'nationally consistent' approaches (Industry Commission 1997a: vii). This must have been a disappointment for the government — given the Prime Minister's wish that such indicators be developed — however, it had neither the constitutional or statutory authority to impose its will on either the state or local governments (Howard 1997).

The second study was organised through the Office of Small Business (the OSB), located in the Department of Industry Tourism and Resources. The OSB worked with line departments and the ORR to develop a set of nine RPIs for the Federal

Government (DITR 2006: 2). Not only was the task intrinsically difficult, there were also contentious issues in relation to the specific objectives of the exercise, such as: the number and type of indicators that should be developed; the potential for overlap with other indicators; the extent to which indicators should be incorporated within a modified RIS process; and, which organisation should be responsible for the indicators. Nevertheless, a set of nine RPI was developed and agreed to by the government. These were designed to provide performance information in relation to the six objectives specified by the Prime Minister (Howard 1997: 82):

- to ensure that all new or revised regulation confers a net benefit on the community;
- to achieve essential regulatory objectives without unduly restricting business in the way in which these objectives are achieved;
- to ensure that the regulatory decision-making processes are transparent and lead to fair outcomes;
- to ensure that information and details on regulation and how to comply with it are accessible and understood by business;
- to create a predictable regulatory environment so business can make decisions with some surety of future environment; and
- to ensure that consultation processes are accessible and responsive to business and the community (DITR 2006: 3-4).

As with the Prime Minister's 1997 statement, this final set of RPI did not contain a specific indicator intended to measure the achievement of a 'lower cost to business' (although this might be estimated from the calculation as to net benefit to the community), or an indicator for administrative efficiency.

The promised study of comparable performance indicators for state and territory governments did not eventuate at this time and no formal explanation has been found by the author for this omission, other than the conclusions of the Productivity Commission report noted above. Officers interviewed indicated that it might have 'fallen between the cracks'. It is worth noting that, in 2006, following the government's acceptance of the *Banks Report*, the Productivity Commission was directed to undertake a study of performance benchmarking for business regulation (Productivity Commission 2006).

Coverage of the indicators

The coverage of the RPI was to be limited to *new* or *modified* primary, secondary or quasi-regulation related directly or indirectly to business and that would have a significant impact on business but excluding tax regulation. While this seemed to neglect both the very large stock of *existing* regulation and the importance of tax regulation — a matter of some concern for all businesses — this was not entirely the case, for all of the Australian governments had agreed to review existing regulation impacting on competition as part of the National Competition Policy review process (Carroll 2006b; Harman 1996). In relation to the exclusion of tax regulation the argument was that public consultation on new or modified taxation measures could be used by taxpayers to avoid or minimise their tax obligations. It was also argued, less convincingly, that it was difficult to assess the impact of specific tax measures in isolation from their implications for the overall tax system (Industry Commission 1997b: 32). The fact that public consultation on new or modified taxes, especially where they might increase the overall tax burden, tends to have negative electoral impacts was not noted, at least in government publications.

The coverage of the RPI was further restricted by applying them only to regulation that was subject to the RIS process managed by the ORR in the year in question (DITR 2006: 4). The RIS process, in turn, excluded regulation of a minor or 'machinery', nature and involved only regulation for which the Federal Government or the Council of Australian Governments (COAG) was responsible, excluding state, territory and local government regulation. The decision to exclude minor and machinery changes in regulation, largely on the grounds of the high administrative costs of reviewing all such regulation, was understandable from the perspective of both the departments and the ORR. However, the exclusion meant that it would not be possible to assess the cost of the cumulative regulatory burden on business — a question of considerable concern for individual businesses and peak associations.

While the considerable restrictions on the coverage of RPI may seem somewhat unreasonable, they were intended to focus the attention of those monitoring and reviewing regulatory performance on performance that was deviating, positively or negatively, from regulatory objectives at an *aggregate*, whole-of-department or whole-of-government level. They were not intended to provide detailed information about regulatory performance at the level of specific regulations, which should be provided, more appropriately, by detailed indicators at the departmental level. As noted above, departments were being encouraged to either introduce, or to improve such detailed indicators at this time in relation to the PBS. While not the topic of this chapter, it should be noted that departments have, in practice, developed and incorporated very few specific RPI within their PBS reports.

An integrated set of regulatory performance indicators

It is clear is that the new system of RPI was not put in place as part of a comprehensive system for measuring regulatory performance. Rather, they were one element in a loosely coordinated set of changes introduced over a period of several years from the later 1990s. The other major changes were: a requirement for annual regulatory plans (the OSB 2003), an improved and somewhat better resourced RIS system (Productivity Commission 1998: 27-8) and the PBS noted above (Department of Finance and Administration 1999). The danger in such a situation is that the information provided by RPI might be considered in isolation from other performance indicators, thereby reducing their value to senior decision-makers, rather than being an important part of an integrated set of indicators enabling more systematic assessments and appropriate, timely, remedial action in relation to regulatory performance. The probability of this occurring was increased with the decision to divide responsibility for the various reform elements among several departments and agencies. Annual regulatory plans were to be developed by departments although, initially, these would be coordinated by the OSB. The annual PBS to be developed by departments, would include appropriate indicators to be reported on in their annual reports. The strengthened RIS was to remain with the ORR. Overall responsibility for the RPI was given to the Office of Small Business, although responsibility for collecting, monitoring and assessing relevant data was split between the ORR (with regard to RPIs 1, 2, 3, 8) and the OSB (RPIs 4, 5, 6, 7, 9), with the ORR providing relevant data to the OSB for collation into an annual report on the RPIs (DITR 2006: 3).

The decision to allocate responsibility for PBS outputs, outcomes and indicators to the departments could hardly have been otherwise, given the extent of the planning task involved and the need for a detailed knowledge of the relevant regulation. However, the decision to split responsibility for RPI between the OSB and the ORR was questionable. On the one hand the ORR was collecting relevant performance data as part of its established RIS process, so it would be inefficient for that to be replicated by the OSB. On the other hand, splitting responsibility for parts of the process increased coordination costs and, possibly, would introduce a degree of friction between the two agencies involved. However, given that the development of RPIs had commenced within the context of small business policy and pressures from small business, it might have been felt that it was politically appropriate to vest at least partial carriage of responsibility for the reform of regulatory systems with the Department of Industry — the department with responsibility for small business policy at the federal level. It is instructive to note that, following a further review of business regulation in 2006, responsibility for RPI was moved from the OSB to a reorganised and renamed ORR, in the shape of the Office of Best Practice Regulation.

The types of RPI

RPI fall into a variety of types, addressing various stages or dimensions of the regulatory process, such as those related to input, process, content, output and outcome. Some indicators provide information about more than one stage, as with RPI 3 and 4 in Table 3.1. The nine RPI put in place were, as Table 1 indicates, very much focused on process, with none directly addressing input, content or outcome and only two addressing output, so that they provided no direct information as to whether or not a regulation was achieving its objectives.

The nine RPIs were defined as follows:

- RPI 1: the proportion of regulations for which the RIS documentation 'adequately addressed net benefit to the community';
- RPI 2: the proportion of regulations for which the RIS adequately justified the compliance burden on business;
- RPI 3: the proportion of regulations which provide businesses and stakeholders with some appropriate flexibility to determine the most cost effective means of achieving regulatory objectives;
- RPI 4: the proportion of cases in which external review of decisions led to a decision being reversed or overturned;
- RPI 5: the proportion of regulatory agencies whose mechanisms for internal review of decisions meet prescribed standards for complaints handling;
- RPI 6: the proportion of regulatory agencies having communications strategies for regulation, or formal consultative channels for communicating information about regulation;
- RPI 7: the proportion of regulatory agencies publishing an adequate forward plan for introduction and review of regulation;
- RPI 8: the proportion of regulations for which the RIS documentation included an adequate statement of consultation; and
- RPI 9: the proportion of regulatory agencies with organisational guidelines outlining consultation processes, procedures and standards.

The lack of outcome-focused indicators is understandable, as it is an inherently difficult task, as the voluminous literature on policy evaluation demonstrates. Also, the primary intent of the reformers at this stage was to improve the quality of the processes involved in making regulation impacting on business, based on the assumption that good regulation-making processes will tend to result in more effective regulation — although they were well aware that good processes did not necessarily lead to good regulation. In retrospect, it is disappointing that the opportunity was not taken to develop at least some outcome indicators, or to at least commence planning for their development. At the least it suggests that, at the time, departments either did not have performance data about regulatory outputs and outcomes, or, if they did possess such data, that it could not be aggregated in a meaningful fashion to provide useful performance information — or, more cynically, that they were fearful that their regulatory performance would be disappointing. Yet, as noted above, the introduction of the PBS system in the same period as the development and introduction of the RPI — with the former's requirement that departments introduce clearly defined outputs, outcomes and related performance indicators, linked to planned and actual expenditures — provided just such an opportunity to develop useful output and outcome indicators.

Table 3.1 Types of RPI

RPIs	Input	Process	Content	Output	Outcome
RPI 1		*			
RPI 2		*			
RPI 3		*		*	
RPI 4		*		*	
RPI 5		*			
RPI 6		*			
RPI 7		*			
RPI 8		*			
RPI 9		*			
Total	0	9	0	2	0

The RPI — performance and practice

In this section the aim is to provide an assessment of the RPI in practice, covering the period from 1998 to 2006. It is divided into a number of sub-sections each of which focuses on one or more of the RPI in relation to the objective in question.

Objective 1: to ensure that all new or revised regulation confers a net benefit on the community

Progress in relation to this objective was measured by RPI 1, the proportion of regulations for which the RIS documentation 'adequately addressed net benefit to the community'. The assessment of the adequacy with which a regulation's net benefit was calculated was the responsibility of the ORR, which then submitted it to the OSB for inclusion in its annual report on RPI. Over the period 1998-99 to 2004-05, the average annual percentage score for all departments and agencies for RPI 1 was 88% , with a range from 81% to 92% (see Table 3.2). It should be noted that the ORR increased the rigour with which it assessed performance over the period, as departments gained familiarity with the RPI, so that it is not possible to compare year to year performance with any degree of precision, although, where the annual performance increased year by year, despite the increased rigour of the assessments, then performance is likely to have increased.

The use of the phrase 'adequately addressed net benefit' in RPI 1, was a clear indication that its designers were well aware of the substantial difficulties involved in costing the likely or actual impact of a regulation. The phrase implies, for example, that cost benefit analysis will be the means for calculating net benefits but it does not specify or require that this must be the case, leaving considerable discretion in the hands of those submitting a proposed regulation to the RIS process. In addition, the use of the word 'adequate', rather than more specific criteria for the assessment of net benefit, enables a wide range of calculations of net benefit, more or less precise, to be judged as 'adequate'. While this might have been realistic, it meant that the value of this measure was distinctly limited for those concerned to see if regulations were likely to achieve a net benefit to the community. It was of somewhat more use for indicating broad trends over time, especially combined with the increasing rigour of the ORR's assessments. Unfortunately, as indicated in Table 3.2, performance as measured by RPI 2 fell somewhat over the period, suggesting that there was no significant improvement in the estimates of net benefit incorporated in the RIS assessed by the ORR.

Table 3.2 Aggregate RPI scores for all agencies, 1998-2005

	No of RIS	RPI 1	RPI 2	RPI 3	RPI 4	RPI 5	RPI 6	RPI 7	RPI 8	RPI 9
1998-99	270	88	91	39	31	77	91	27	92	59
1999-0	225	92	94	77	61	67	100	47	96	74
2000-1	167	92	92	66	70	50	100	73	91	68
2001-02	225	92	94	77	61	67	100	47	96	74
2002-03	139	81	85	82	70	65	88	70	87	58
2003-04	115	91	91	86	62	75	95	76	91	48
2004-05	83	82	81	100	58	72	89	78	82	56
Average	175	88	90	75	59	68	95	60	91	62

Source: the OSB Annual Reports 1998-99 to 2004-05

In practice, the ORR in its publication *A Guide to Regulation*, did specify the type of costs and benefits to be included by departments in their RIS documentation. It noted that there were considerable difficulties in gaining precise, quantitative estimates of costs and benefits but encouraged departments to at least identify and, where possible, assess the fullest range of costs and benefits, although admitting that quantification was not always possible or necessary — although the onus of proof was on the department to defend the lack of quantification (the ORR 1998: D10).

Hence, it was quite possible that the ORR might judge the calculation of net benefit in an RIS as 'adequate', even where little or no quantitative data or assessment was included. If those relying on such performance data were aware of such limitations, it could be argued that at least it gave a rather crude, largely qualitative indicator of some value, although the lack of an upward trend in performance over the period was disappointing. However, even this limited value has to be questioned as, in practice, what was reported in the annual OSB report was only that proportion of a department's regulations judged as 'adequate' in the year in question, in the form of a simple percentage figure, for example, 75%, with very little further explanation or clarification. Further, given that in any one year a department might have submitted only one or two RIS, then the value of providing a percentage indicator as a measure of performance was of questionable value for senior decision-makers and, of course, for Parliament, business and the community.

Objective 2: to achieve essential regulatory objectives without unduly restricting business in the way in which these objectives are achieved

Objective 2 was measured by two indicators, RPI 2 — the proportion of regulations for which the RIS adequately justified the compliance burden on business — and RPI 3 — the proportion of regulations which provide businesses and stakeholders with some appropriate flexibility to determine the most cost effective means of achieving regulatory objectives — both to be monitored by the ORR. Over the period 1998-99 to 2004-05, the average annual percentage score for all departments and agencies for RPI 2 was 90%, with a range of 81% to 94%, and for RPI 3 was 75%, with a very large range of 39% to 100%. While the average of 90% for RPI 2 might have been reassuring, in the three years previous there was an increased variation with regard to the annual performance, to a low of 81% in 2004-05, which was of concern. In contrast, performance in relation to RPI 3 increased dramatically over the period, even with the increase in the rigour of the ORR's assessments. Unfortunately the OSB annual reports provide no indication as to why performance improved (or fell), for any of the indicators.

If, as indicated above, it was difficult to provide accurate estimates of the costs and benefits of proposed regulation, then RPI 2 at least required departments to provide clear, logical arguments to support their proposals and (perhaps) to think through the compliance implications for business. If backed up by accurate, quantitative estimates of compliance costs and benefits, so much the better. In practice, its value, as with RPI 1, was limited by the lack of specific criteria against which adequacy would be judged (although the ORR did provide advice to departments in this regard) and the lack of quantitative estimates provided in practice by departments. As the ORR's annual reports very clearly indicate, departmental estimates of regulatory costs and benefits were often unsatisfactory. Indeed, the Chairman of the Productivity Commission (of which the ORR is a unit), Gary Banks, indicated that in 2004 only 20% of tabled RISs contained even an attempt at quantifying the costs related to proposed regulations (Banks 2005: 10). If Banks was correct in his estimate, then it is difficult to see how, for example, 82% of all regulations assessed in 2004-05 could be assessed as adequate in relation to RPI 1 and 81% in relation to RPI 2 despite the fact that 20% of all RIS did not even attempt to quantify the costs related to the proposed regulations (the OSB 2006:38). It suggests a very flexible interpretation as to the meaning of adequacy and, importantly, makes the value of both RPI very questionable as reliable measures of regulatory performance.

RPI 3 was based on whether or not a department's RIS contained any one or more of the following measures:

- a performance or outcome based standard which did not prescribe how a business was to comply with the standard;
- provision for a business to seek acceptance of an alternative mechanism for achieving compliance than that prescribed in the regulation;
- the use of a market-based mechanism such as tradeable permits to allow businesses flexibility in determining a compliance strategy; and
- offered a range of means for businesses to have flexibility in deciding what steps to take in compliance (Department of Industry Tourism and Resources 2006: 14).

While the intent of RPI 3 is clear — being a measure of the degree of flexibility that a proposed regulation allows businesses in their compliance with regulation — the assumption it contains of the attractiveness of regulatory flexibility to business is problematical. A small business, for example, has limited resources of both money and time. Hence, the use of those resources to determine how it should comply with a regulatory performance or outcome based standard, rather than simply complying in a way prescribed in a regulation, is not necessarily attractive. At the least, it requires the business to design an appropriate strategy, or to purchase a ready-made strategy, or to employ a consultant to design the strategy. Faced with such choices, how many small businesses would not welcome a helpful regulatory prescription as to the required strategy, assuming the prescription is cost effective and meets compliance needs?

In summary, RPI 2 and 3 provided a rather mixed message for decision-makers, suggesting that regulations were providing an increase in the flexibility with which businesses could comply with regulations but, worryingly, a decline in the extent to which departments provided an adequate justification for the regulations in question. When the trend for RPI 2 is combined with the downward trend in RPI 1 — performance related to the calculation of net benefits — it suggests, if rather speculatively, that the efforts of the ORR and the OSB to encourage departments to improve regulatory quality in these important dimensions was unsuccessful, despite their increased efforts owing to a boost to their resources following the *Bell Report*.

Objective 3: to ensure that the regulatory decision-making processes are transparent and lead to fair outcomes

This was to be measured by RPI 4 — the proportion of cases in which external review of decisions (as defined) led to a decision being reversed or overturned — and RPI 5 — the proportion of regulatory agencies whose mechanisms for internal review of decisions meet standards for complaints handling outlined in 'Principles for Developing a Service Charter' published by the Department of Finance and Administration. Departments and agencies were to provide the relevant information to the OSB for inclusion in its annual report. Over the period

1998-999 to 2004-05, the average annual percentage score for all departments and agencies for RPI 4 was 59%, with a range from 31% to 70%, but a declining trend from 2002-03. This was a disturbingly poor level of performance. The average annual score for RPI 5 was 68%, with a range from 50% to 77%, with a slight upwards trend in the latter three years, following an initial and very sharp fall in performance. In the case of RPI 5, where departments had only to meet the standards for complaints handling quite clearly specified by the Department of Finance and Administration, the average score of 68% was surprisingly low.

Unlike RPI 1 to 3, RPI 4 focused attention on the performance of departments in administering regulations. In particular, departments were assessed on their adherence to due process rather than administrative efficiency. The assumption was that if the proportion of cases where a decision was reversed or overturned by an external body was low, then the quality of the decision process, at least with regard to due process, was relatively high. While there is no doubt that RPI 4 might provide a valuable, more objective indicator of due process performance, two limitations need to be considered: one, limitations as to the sources of external decisions to be considered and reported upon; two, small business resource limitations.

With regard to the sources of external decisions to be included, the formal advice to departments was that they should only consider decisions of external review agencies that were empowered to overturn or reverse the department's decision (Department of Industry Tourism and Resources 2006: 7-8). This meant that, for example, complaints from businesses to the Commonwealth Ombudsman would not be considered, even if the Ombudsman supported the complaint, as the Ombudsman had no power to overturn or reverse decisions. In addition, decisions resulting from departments' internal review processes were excluded, even if they supported the complainant. In this latter case, while a degree of concern as to the objectivity of reviews from internal review sources is not surprising, it is surprising that they were not to be considered, even, for example, where they might have led to the overturning of an earlier decision. If they had been included as a source of performance data, this might have encouraged departments to adopt internal review processes where they did not exist and, where they did exist and indicated poor levels of performance, to improve their procedures and related decisions, especially if such information was made public in the RPI reports.

The second limitation springs from the limited resources small businesses have to take complaints about regulation and its implementation to external review bodies such as the courts or the Administrative Review Tribunal. Faced with this reality, the decision to exclude from consideration those decisions overturned within the potentially less costly and less formal internal review processes of departments was unduly restrictive. In part, the impact of this restriction might have been mitigated by RPI 5, the proportion of regulatory agencies whose mechanisms for internal review of decisions met standards for complaints handling outlined in the *Principles for Developing a Service Charter*. Some 12 criteria had to be satisfied in order to meet these standards, as determined by the Department of Finance and Administration (Department of Industry Tourism and Resources 2006: 8-9). The assumption was that if a department's processes satisfied these criteria then it was likely that its internal processes were at least adequate insofar as complainants were concerned. Thus, departments were required only to answer 'yes' or 'no' with regard to RPI 5 and to provide a brief description of their internal review processes in their first report but not thereafter. It hardly needs pointing out that having sound processes does not guarantee good decisions and, given that the average annual score for all departments for the whole period for RPI 5 was only 68% (on a self-declared basis) then there is room for legitimate concern as to the adequacy of departmental performance in ensuring transparency or fair outcomes — the very objective measured by RPI 4 and 5.

Objective 4: to ensure that information and details on regulation and how to comply with it are accessible and understood by business

This was to be measured by RPI 6 — the proportion of regulatory agencies having communications strategies for regulation, or formal consultative channels for communicating information about regulation. Over the period 1998-99 to 2004-05 the average annual percentage score for all departments and agencies for RPI 6 was 95%, with an initially impressive performance falling away somewhat after 2001-02.

Departments and agencies provided: a simple 'yes' or 'no' answer to the question of whether they had communication strategies or formal consultative channels; a brief description of the strategy or channels in question; and, where the department had a formal, written strategy, a copy of that document was submitted to the OSB. Where such strategies existed but had not been in place for the full reporting period, departments were advised to answer 'yes' to the question (Department of Industry Tourism and Resources 2006: 11). In practice, there seems to have been no little or no checking by either the ORR or the OSB as to whether the strategies or consultative channels actually enabled businesses to access and understand information on regulations other than as demonstrated in relation to RPI 8 and 9, below. In other words the value of RPI 6 was limited, focusing only on the achievement of procedural targets rather than any assessment of whether or not businesses found the consultative channels accessible or the information provided about regulations understandable. However, assuming that adequate processes might encourage accessibility and understanding, then an average performance level of 95% for the period was reassuring, even with the slight downward trend after 2001-02.

Objective 5: to create a predictable regulatory environment so business can make decisions with some surety of future environment

This was to be measured by RPI 7, the proportion of regulatory agencies publishing an adequate forward plan for introduction and review of regulation. Departments and agencies were to provide the relevant information to the OSB for inclusion in its annual report. Over the period 1998-99 to 2004-05, the average annual percentage score for all departments and agencies for RPI 7 was only 60%, with a range from 27% to 78%, although some reassurance could be gained from the consistently upward trend in performance after 2001-02. In other words, assuming that this RPI did provide a reliable indicator as to the 'surety of future environment', there was a substantial lack of surety for those businesses affected by the 40% of regulatory agencies that did not publish an adequate forward plan in the period under consideration. In addition, the extent to which such a predictable regulatory environment can be anticipated on the basis of a business knowing that a regulatory review is planned, is questionable, given that the planned reviews could result in substantial change, with at least short term uncertainty.

Objective 6: to ensure that consultation processes are accessible and responsive to business and the community

This was to be measured by RPI 8, the proportion of regulations for which the RIS documentation included an adequate statement of consultation (to be monitored and assessed by the ORR) and RPI 9, the proportion of regulatory agencies with organisational guidelines outlining consultation processes, procedures and standards, with departments and agencies to provide the relevant information to the OSB for inclusion in its annual report. In part, RPI 8 and 9 overlap with RPI 4, above, providing additional information as to the adequacy of consultation processes, based on the assessment by the ORR of the documentation provided in the RIS process. Over the period 1998-99 to 2004-05, the average annual percentage score for all departments and agencies for RPI 8 was 91%, with a range from 82% to 96%, but a worrying, downward trend from 2001-02, to a figure of 82% in 2004-05. The average annual score for RPI 9 was only 62%, with a range from 48% to 74% and a downward trend after 2001-02. Again, RPI 8 and 9 provide performance information only in relation to departmental processes, not their actual impact on business, that is, whether they actually result in accessibility and responsiveness. Hence, given that the average level of process performance for RPI 9 was only 62%, one might speculate that the actual accessibility and responsiveness of consultation processes used by departments was of a rather low order, both for business and the community.

Conclusion

In summary, the performance information provided by the nine RPI for the period under consideration was certainly interesting, of varying degrees of value and, for RPI 3 and 7, showed improving regulatory performance by departments and agencies. The other RPI, however, suggested that regulatory performance in relation to process was at best variable and as indicated for several RPI, in a downward trend. Combined with the coverage and design limitations noted above, they indicate that the Australian system of RPI, while a step forward, was of limited value. Perhaps of most concern for proponents of regulatory reform, its limited success suggested that the decades-long effort to improve the international competitiveness of the Australian economy by improving the capacity of regulation-making processes to reject anti-competitive, regulatory proposals, had been of only very limited success.

References

ACCI 2005a, 'Holding Back the Red Tape Avalanche: A Regulatory Reform Agenda for Australia', Position Paper, November.

— 2005b, 'Modern Workplace: Safer Workplace — An Australian Industry Blueprint for Improving Health and Safety', April.

Australian Government 2006, *Rethinking Regulation Report of the Taskforce on Reducing Regulatory Burdens on Business — Australian Government's Response*, as at 2 October 2006, at http://www.treasury.gov.au/contentitem.asp?ContentID=1141&NavID=

Banks, G. 2003a, *Reducing the business costs of regulation*, March, Productivity Commission, as at 12 June 2006, at http://www.pc.gov.au/speeches/cs20030320/index.html

— 2003b, *The good, the bad and the ugly: economic perspectives on regulation in Australia*, 2 October, Productivity Commission, as at 12 June 2006, at http://www.pc.gov.au/speeches/cs20031002/index.html

— 2004, *NCP and beyond: an agenda for national reform*, 6 December, Productivity Commission, as at 12 June 2006, at http://www.pc.gov.au/speeches/cs20041206/index.html

— 2005, *Regulation-making in Australia: Is it broke? How do we fix it?* A public lecture at the ANU as part of the Public Lecture Series of the Australian Centre of Regulatory Economics (ACORE) and the Faculty of Economics and Commerce, ANU, Canberra, 7 July. As at 7 February 2007, at http://www.pc.gov.au/speeches/cs20050707/index.html

— 2006, *Rethinking Regulation*, January, as at 12 June 2006, at http://www.regulationtaskforce.gov.au/index.html

BCA 2005a, *Locking in or Losing Prosperity — Australia's Choice*, Business Council of Australia, as at 12 June 2006, at http://www.bca.com.au/content.asp?newsID=99077

BCA 2005b, *Business Regulation Action Plan for Future Prosperity*, Business Council of Australia, as at 28 June 2006, at http://www.bca.com.au/content.asp?newsID=99099

Carroll, P. 2006a, 'Regulatory Impact Analysis: promise and reality', a refereed paper presented to the Australasian Political Studies conference, University of Newcastle 25-27 September 2006.

— 2006b, 'National politics, Regulatory Reform and Intergovernmental Relations: the Australian case', a paper presented to the European Group of Public Administration conference, 6-9 September 2006, Bocconi University, Milan.

Department of Finance and Administration 1999, *Specifying Outcomes and Outputs: The Commonwealth's Accrual-based Outcomes and Outputs Framework and Outcomes and Outputs: Guidance for Review*, Department of Finance and Administration, Canberra.

— 2007, *Performance Reporting Under Outcomes and Outputs*, as at 5 February 2007, at http://www.finance.gov.au/budgetgroup/Commonwealth_Budget_-Overview/performance_reporting.html

Department of Industry, Tourism and Resources 2006, *Regulatory Performance Indicators A Guide for Departments and Agencies*, DITR, Canberra.

Department of the Prime Minister and Cabinet 2007, *Requirements for Annual Reports for Departments, Executive Agencies and FMA ACT Bodies*, Department of the Prime Minister and Cabinet, as at 5 February 2007, at http://www.dpmc.gov.au/guidelines/docs/annual_report_requirements.pdf

Harman, E. 1996, 'The National Competition Policy: A study of the Policy Process and Network', *Australian Journal of Political Science*, Vol 31, No. 2, pp. 205-223.

Head, B. and E. McCoy (eds) 1991, *Deregulation or Better Regulation?*, Macmillan, South Melbourne.

Howard, J. 1997, *More Time for Business*, AGPS, Canberra.

Industry Commission 1993, *Developments in Regulation and its Review, 1992/3'*, Industry Commission, AGPS, as at 12 June 2006, at http://www.pc.gov.au/orr/reports/annrpt/reglnrev9293/index.html

Industry Commission 1997a, *Performance Measures for Councils Improving Local Government Performance Indicators*, Research Report, Industry Commission, as at 6 February 2007, at http://www. pc.gov.au/ic/research/independent/localgov/finalreport/ localgov.pdf

Industry Commission 1997b, *Regulation and its Review 1996-97*, AusInfo, Canberra.

OECD 2004a, *Regulatory Performance: Ex-Post Evaluation of Regulatory Tools and Institutions,* OECD, Paris.

OECD 2004b, *Regulatory Impact Analysis (RIA) Inventory*, OECD, Paris.

ORR 1998, *A Guide to Regulation*, second edition.

OSB 1999, *Regulatory Performance Indicators Report from the Office of Small Business for the Financial Year 1998-999*, Office of Small Business, Canberra.

— 2003, *Annual Regulatory Plans Guidelines for agencies on preparing and publishing regulatory plans*, Office of Small Business, May, Canberra.

— 2006, *Encouraging Enterprise*, Office of Small Business, Canberra.

Productivity Commission 1998, *Regulation and its Review 1997–98*, AusInfo, Canberra.

— 2006, *Terms of Reference*, as at 16 February 2007, at http://www.pc.gov.au/study/regulationbenchmarking/tor.html

— 2007, *Performance Benchmarking of Australian Business Regulation*, as at 25 February, at http://www.pc.gov.au/study/regulationbenchmarking /index.html

SBDTF 1996, *Time for Business*, Commonwealth of Australia.

Chapter 4. The mirage of rail reform: building regulatory capacity in policy sectors

Chris Walker

Introduction

The title of this chapter is somewhat provocative and is intended to focus attention on the question of whether or not regulatory reform in Australia is only about cutting red tape and achieving national consistency. My experience as a state government official for some 15 years, in both line and central agencies, suggests that there exists a dominant view that regulatory reform will only deliver value when it is about achieving simplicity and consistency. This appears to be the orthodox view across all governments at both Commonwealth and state levels. There is, of course, considerable value in creating regulatory environments that are simple and easy to follow for all participants. In a federal structure, for example, where inter-jurisdictional transactions and cross border services operate, treating these activities in a consistent manner makes sense for the organisations and individuals concerned. However, one of the keys for successfully managing organisations within the modern world is about building the capacity to operate and work within complex regulatory systems. As Quiggin (2006) claims, innovation and diversity are more enduring than neat and tidy arrangements based on uniformity and simplicity. If we are to achieve the capacity to operate complex systems then we need systems that enable organisations to effectively operate within those diverse and complex regulatory environments.

The argument that follows is similar to the position put forward by Twomey and Withers in their recent paper on Australian federalism (2007). They argue that reform efforts should focus on working within our system of governance to improve our capacity to reallocate roles and responsibilities and improve mechanisms of intergovernmental cooperation. Their argument suggests that rather than work only to reduce complicated arrangements and diversity, governments should also work to harness the benefits of federalism. This will result, they argue, in more flexible and responsive government, promoting innovation and efficiency through competition (Twomey and Withers 2007:6).

The chapter is divided into six sections, followed by a conclusion. The first examines what is meant by expanding the regulatory reform process to include building regulatory capacity across policy sectors. The second looks at the increasing trend to a centralisation of decision-making in Australia's federal system. The third analyses some of the negative impacts associated with the use of targets as a means for regulatory reform. The fourth and fifth sections, following Steane and Carroll, suggest that, in practice, regulatory systems necessarily are becoming more complex, not less, despite the waves of regulatory reform that have occurred. The sixth section examines the case of the National Transport Commission (NTC) in relation to regulatory reform in land transport.

Regulatory reform and capacity building

Regulatory systems involve two key elements, the process of regulation-making and the instruments and approaches required for compliance and enforcement (Doern 2003). Recent Australian debate on regulatory reform (Regulation Taskforce 2006) has predominately focussed on the second component with the objective of simplifying instruments of enforcement, for example, proposing a movement from traditional, prescriptive regulation, to various models of industry self regulation. It also stresses the need to streamline regulatory systems by, for example, removing duplication of effort across levels of government and achieving regulatory uniformity. In summary, the key demands from industry and governments have been that we need to reduce the level of regulation and simplify what remains.

There is no doubt pressure needs to be maintained to ensure regulatory systems are responsive and adaptive to change. Regulatory frameworks need to be under constant review in order to ensure unnecessary regulation is removed and where appropriate more innovative and responsive mechanisms introduced. However, policy makers also need to monitor, evaluate and improve how participants in a regulatory sector function within complex systems. In particular, the central agencies of government have an important role to play in assessing whether the institutional arrangements and regulatory mechanisms within particular policy sectors facilitate and develop the capacity of businesses, non government organisations and key public sector agencies to participate in the policy-making process and achieve higher levels of regulatory compliance.

In a globalised world markets are becoming more complex and interdependent. Local standards, rules and operating procedures are increasingly influenced by national and international forces that aim to more seamlessly integrate the efficient movement of goods and services across national boundaries, free from unnecessary and varying, regulatory requirements. The result is a proliferation of international trade agreements and the increasing development of international standards, accompanied, at the national level by processes of mutual recognition, harmonisation and the adoption of Australian Standards aimed at regulatory simplification.

There is also mounting pressure to further integrate and build relationships across related systems. Those responsible for the regulation of the freight rail sector, for example, now take a stronger interest in how its operations interface with road and sea transport systems. As COAG notes: 'More flexible rules governing access to the road network should be established that will allow freight carried by rail to be seamlessly picked up and dropped off by road transport operations.' (COAG 2006: Appendix C:14). The result is increasing regulatory harmonisation, as well as an increasing harmonisation of, for example, communication systems across transport modes, such as standardised electronic tracking systems for containers and goods. These systems are then 'overlayed', by other regulatory regimes such as those related to OH&S and the environment. In terms of Doern's analysis of regulatory regimes (2003), we see sectoral regulatory issues specific to rail interacting with broader 'horizontal' framework regulatory regimes that are universally applied across a range of policy fields. This interaction of regulation, standards and rules that have both specific and universal impact on policy sectors adds to the complexity of policy, building a layered regulatory framework into the system of governance.

It is this constantly changing and overlapping nature of regulatory systems that suggests that the debate on regulatory reform should be expanded to include strategies that enhance the capacity of agencies and stakeholders to better manage and respond to this increasing regulatory complexity. This is an issue of genuine concern for line agencies heavily involved in regulation, where the dominant discourse focuses on reducing the burden of red tape and the causes of over-regulation but neglects the need to build and improve the capacity to cope with regulatory complexity. The issue of building capacity to manage and operate within a diverse and ever changing regulatory environment has received little attention from central agencies and COAG. In their discourse, regulation is still regarded with some suspicion and efforts to promote a positive agenda of working *with* regulation are less likely to be vigorously supported (McConkey and Dutil 2006). What is necessary is the introduction into Australian jurisdictions of 'Capability Reviews', similar to those being undertaken of key government departments in the United Kingdom (Cabinet Office 2006). These reviews examine current and future demands on departments and look at their capacity to manage and respond to changing circumstances and demands. The reviews are focussed on future needs and examine how customers and stakeholders are engaged in the design and management of service delivery and the related regulatory models. An examination of regulatory capability might also involve extending the assessment of an agency's capability to include an assessment of the overall capacity of the sector. Such a review would look at the constraints or barriers for key participants (public and private) to successfully engage and comply with regulatory arrangements that govern behaviour and the rules of operation and engagement.

Many commentators have observed an incremental centralisation of regulatory reform agendas over recent years (Quiggin 2006; Patty 2006). The recent High

Court decision on Commonwealth powers in respect to industrial relations saw a flurry of commentary expressing concern with the growing centralisation of Commonwealth power and the need to reform the federation (Debus 2006; Lynch 2006; Dick 2006). Twomey and Withers (2007) present a comprehensive argument as to what they regard as the negative economic and social consequences of such centralisation of power in the Australian federation. A key theme is their concern with what they see as a growing Commonwealth interest in the detail of policy, an area that has traditionally been managed by states. This is a process Twomey and Withers refer to as 'opportunistic federalism' (2007: 5) and is evident in the shifting of COAG's interest from system wide issues of institutional arrangements to more specific reform targets that shape the rules and patterns of interaction on matters of detail in various policy sectors. In this context, the Commonwealth, drawing on its authority and financial strength, has shaped the COAG agenda to reflect its increasingly centralised, political and policy interests (Twomey and Withers 2007). COAG's focus on detail seems to have distracted it from the more strategic issue of how regulatory institutions and processes of governance influence the operational capacity and compliance levels of stakeholders and participants in key policy sectors.

In land transport, as in other sectors, there exist well established systems for handling the detailed matters of inter-jurisdictional coordination and cooperation, such as Ministerial Councils and their supporting forums of chief executives from government agencies. In the late 1980s and early 1990s pressure for microeconomic reform saw heads of government become increasingly involved in steering inter-jurisdictional reform agendas in several key policy sectors. In land transport, for example, central agencies and, ultimately, COAG, took a strong lead in shaping institutional arrangements for regulatory reform, leading to the 1991 Intergovernmental Agreement that established the National Road Transport Commission (NRTC) (Painter 1998). However, what is important to note is that while central agencies were critical in pushing the establishment of the NRTC, they did not shape the details of the reform agenda and resulting work. This arose out of the detailed work and proposals of the various road and transport agencies (Wilson and Moore 2006). The success of the NRTC as a model for progressing regulatory reform was acknowledged in 2004 when its mandate was expanded to include rail and it was renamed the National Transport Commission (NTC).

However, in 2006, COAG once again became involved in land transport reform but this time announcing a far more detailed approach to reform with a set of specific targets and timelines. In particular, it requested the simplification of rail safety regulation by December 2006, with a program of work specifically targeting accreditation guidelines, safety management system requirements, disclosure of information and the management of fatigue amongst rail workers (NTC 2006). This recent interest by heads of government in the operational detail of policy represents a shift from the 1991 approach, where the focus was on developing appropriate institutions and accompanying frameworks for progressing reform, not operational detail. It also continues to neglect the question of improving our regulatory capacity to deal with complex systems.

The problem with targets in complex systems

A significant risk in setting a program of reform with specified targets, such as that proposed by COAG for rail safety regulation, is that it focuses agency interest on delivering a 'one-off', result at one point in time rather than in creating incentives for embedding ongoing processes of quality improvement and review. For example, achieving national consistency in the regulation of rail sidings by December 2006, for inclusion in a report to COAG, tends to focus activity on reaching uniformity rather than any real assessment of the best approach for regulating the access and safety management systems of such facilities. The challenge of revising existing operational systems and practices within set timeframes means that jurisdictions tend to add each other's requirements together to build a common national approach rather than review practices down to the minimum most effective requirement. National targets tend to result in the mere 'compilation', of practices rather than a rigorous identification of the most effective and efficient approach. It suggests that we have stable, static, regulatory and operational systems that can be reduced to a set of simple regulatory requirements. Specifying targets also tends to lead to the neglect of areas not included on the list of targets for reform and action. Rather, reform efforts should acknowledge the dynamic nature of the regulatory process and the complexity of systems and also focus on means to enable participants to more effectively deal with and manage that complexity. An unwarranted assumption that simplicity can be achieved distracts from the need to develop an understanding of the processes of regulatory transformation that are currently underway across many policy sectors.

The case of rail freight is an illustrative example. The microeconomic reform efforts of governments during the 1980s and 1990s saw rail systems undergo massive transformations. Independent, localised networks that were government owned and integrated both vertically and horizontally within states were transformed into a more complex set of arrangements of public, corporatised and privatised operations (Productivity Commission 1999:92). The transformation of railways from single, state owned entities in the 1990s to a multi-organisational arena with both public and private participants, subject to independent regulatory oversight, clearly demonstrates the growing diversity and complexity of policy sectors, even though the initial reform aim may have been to gain greater harmonisation and regulatory simplicity. The result is that the shaping of public policy in relation to railways has become a much more complicated, multilayered process for organisations and individuals, managers and politicians, as suggested by Steane and Carroll (2001).

Out of this process of change two key outcomes can be observed. Firstly, a growing desire amongst some participants and observers to simplify arrangements, including further regulatory reform. The increased complexity in railway systems brought about, at least in part, by the wave of reforms in the 1990s, is now seen by some as a cost to business and a potential constraint on operational efficiency (Regulation Taskforce 2006). Second, the process of making and modifying regulation has become more porous and complex, with a broader range of public and private participants gaining access to and varying degrees of influence upon, policy networks and forums. This is evident, for example, in relation to COAG, where a wider range of economic interests has entered the regulatory reform debate, bringing pressure to bear as to the need to engage in detailed reform of rail safety regulation. Nor is this phenomenon confined to Australia. Doern (2006), for example, suggests that in federal systems operating with multiple levels of governance there is evidence of increasing pressure to merge, collapse or rationalise previously separate levels of regulation. He argues that this tendency is mainly driven by business interests promoting a neo-liberal agenda primarily concerned with economic productivity. It is ironic that those interests are now calling for freer markets, smaller government and regulatory simplicity, when it was, in large part, similar calls for microeconomic reform that resulted in the break up, privatisation and expansion of regulation in the Australian rail sector in the 1990s.

The growing complexity of regulation and policy sectors

A key observation of the Regulation Taskforce was that there had been a proliferation of regulatory agencies across all levels of government. It argued that these agencies, along with their excessive regulatory output, have added further layers to the policy process and increased the complexity of regulation (Banks 2005; Regulation Taskforce 2006). The OECD (2002) has made similar observations and argues that governments now need to work to simplify regulatory systems. This is an increased focus on the quality and value of regulation and 'whether the legitimate policy goals underlying the regulation can be achieved in a way that does not impose as high a burden on business' (Regulation Taskforce 2006:2).

Regulators and policy makers have had to skill up to deal with the changing nature of the policy and institutional environment. Regulatory agencies no longer operate as traditional pubic sector bureaucracies in stable environments where the organisation's tasks are highly specified, discrete and carried out on a routine basis (Considine 2005). The complexity of the tasks and the environment in which regulators now work means staff need to exercise judgment and respond with innovative solutions to problems as they emerge. Regulatory agencies need to be adaptive organisations responding to business demands and environmental changes.

Steane and Carroll (2001), in reviewing the early work of the OECD on regulatory reform, are critical of its argument that what is emerging and what is needed, is a new regulatory state. In particular, they note that a key OECD report reveals an expectation that the state 'will be less intrusive, with other social systems, notably markets providing the dynamic that will drive society. The state will not 'wither away' but will become an 'umpire', adjudicating with regard to transgressions of the rules.' (Steane and Carroll 2001:33). They take issue with this argument, suggesting that, in an environment of multiple networks of contracts and public private partnerships, the task of governance becomes more challenging as smaller public sector agencies work to influence and manage more complex arrangements of inter-organisational relations (2001:39). It is, they suggest, the need to manage this complexity that is now a major challenge for government agencies and key stakeholders as they work to navigate, influence and participate in the policy process.

The challenge of building innovation and flexibility into regulatory regimes

A recent report on harmonisation in the Australian rail industry (BTRE 2006) notes the difficulty of balancing the benefits of uniformity with customised arrangements for localised operations. The report notes that in complex technical systems like railways, with a relatively small number of operators, the potential for regulators to adopt customised systems is far more likely. Combine this with the Australian federal structure of decision-making and the potential for achieving uniformity in some areas of regulation become almost impossible. In fact the report states:

> The regulatory track record in Australia in the last decade is one of regulatory instability. Since the establishment of State regulatory bodies in the 1990s, the regulators have sought to maintain consistency. Despite the signing of intergovernmental agreements on 'rail safety' and on 'rail operational uniformity' (in 1996 and 1999, respectively), jurisdictional safety regulators continued to develop safety regulations on an individual basis. Regulatory systems diverged from the outset (BTRE 2006: XXV).

Failure to achieve uniformity however, is not all bad news. Developments in regulatory techniques and compliance technology now mean that jurisdictions are developing the capacity to manage and regulate for variable standards of performance within similar industries. The focus of regulatory enforcement is moving away from prescriptive rules to outcomes and performance-based standards. Innovation in approaches to regulation requires both the industry and government agencies to have an informed understanding of regulation and greater capability to work within complex regulatory regimes. How do we get such regulatory innovation to prosper in a climate of reform that remains focussed on the rhetoric of deregulation, red tape reduction and a preference for simple prescriptive consistency?

The National Transport Commission (NTC) as a model for capacity building

It is in this context that the experience and practices of the NTC are worth reviewing. This institutional model demonstrates the value of linking sector wide capacity building with reform programs. While the primary function of the NTC is to promote uniform regulation in land transport the Commission's influence and approach to its work also develops industry and government capacity to work more effectively in an ever changing regulatory environment. The Commission plays a key role in shaping industry opinion and attitudes towards reform and regulation (Painter 1998:146).

The NTC experience demonstrates that as well as supporting uniformity there are times where industry concerns centre on the lack of flexibility and capacity of regulation to account for local variation and need. There is a desire for regulatory regimes to accommodate two opposing views:

*   consistent treatment of all participants under uniform systems and requirements; and
*   a capacity to accommodate variation based on local circumstances.

The NTC has developed a culture of cooperative decision-making in the development of land transport policy and regulatory reform (Wilson and Moore 2006:298). It has an extensive range of consultation mechanisms and this includes regulatory authorities, transport agencies, enforcement agencies and representatives from the road and rail industry. The effectiveness of the NTC model rests in its robust policy development process, one that engages transport ministers and links their decisions on reform to a broad intergovernmental agreement that commits governments to a reform process. It is also a participative process, with substantial input from industry advisory bodies, ensuring a broad range of stakeholders are engaged and have access to the process.

Since its inception in 1992 the Commission has progressed regulatory reform in a range of areas impacting on land transport. This has included driver licensing regulations, vehicle standards, emission standards, vehicle registration regulations and legislation governing compliance and enforcement arrangements. The Commission's current approach to the development and implementation of the new national rail safety laws involves communication strategies, provision of information and guidelines and working groups aimed at helping parties in the rail industry to comply with the legislative requirements. In preparing for the implementation of new rail safety regulation the NTC has also looked at how reform will be maintained into the future. This action is more about building and sustaining regulatory and compliance capacity in the sector. Their work includes the release of an information package for stakeholders that explains how states and territories will work together to ensure regulatory consistency (NTC 2006:2).

The Commission has also recommended changes to the institutional arrangements for the administration of rail safety regulatory regimes. This includes:

- establishing development and approval processes for national guidelines and codes;
- detailing processes for the maintenance and review of legislation, regulations and guideline material; and
- establishing administrative arrangements for the recognition of industry codes and standards (NTC 2006).

It is this type of analysis that reform agendas should aim to promote but tend to neglect. The work of the NTC in rail safety recognises the need to develop mechanisms to more effectively manage complex systems for the benefit of governments, industry and the community (NTC 2004). While not an explicit role of the organisation, the Commission's work in developing regulations has a major influence on the understanding stakeholders have of the regulatory framework within which they operate. The consultative work of the NTC brings industry and government into the regulatory development process and jointly builds their understanding of what is a dynamic regulatory environment. The outcome is an improvement in both regulation-making and compliance in the land transport sector.

Conclusion

The governing of policy in a federal system increasingly involves complex systems of state and non-state actors and we need to rethink our approach to regulatory reform to include the building of sector wide capacity to effectively operate within such complex and dynamic environments. An advantage of our federal system is that it enables local variation to meet local needs, responding with a degree of sensitivity to pressures at a variety of levels of government. It provides an admittedly complex set of state based and nationally based consultative forums. In land transport reform the National Transport Commission is a key player in this process, both enabling differing interests to have a voice, as well as playing an essential part in guiding and managing, as an independent body, what is a necessarily complex system.

References

Banks, G. 2005, *Regulation –making in Australia: Is it broke? How do we fix it?*, Productivity Commission, viewed 9 October 2007, http://www.pc.gov.au/speeches/cs20050707/index.html

Banks, G. 2006a, *Reducing the regulatory burden: the way forward*, Productivity Commission, viewed 9 October 2007, http://www.pc.gov.au/speeches/cs20060517/index.html

Banks, G. 2006b, *Tackling the underlying causes of over-regulation: an update*, Productivity Commission, viewed 9 October 2007, http://www.pc.gov.au/speeches/cs20061024/index.html

Banks, G. 2006c, *Regulation for Australia's Federation in the 21st Century*. Productivity Commission, viewed 9 October 2007, http://www.pc.gov.au/speeches/cs20061103/index.html

BTRE 2006, Optimising harmonisation in the Australian railway industry. Report 114, BTRE, Canberra.

Cabinet Office 2006, *Capability Reviews: The findings of the first four reviews*. United Kingdom Cabinet Office, London.

Considine, M. 2005, *Making Public Policy*, Polity Press, Cambridge.

Council of Australian Governments 2006, Communiqué, February, viewed 14 February 2006, http://www.coag.gov.au/

Debus, B. 2006, 'States left out on a limb as the Commonwealth's power increases', *Sydney Morning Herald*, 16 November.

Deegan, M. 2006, *Twice the task: Transport in the information age*, Speech by the NTC Acting Chairman, 14 February, National Transport Commission, Melbourne.

Dick, T. 2006, 'High noon for the States', *Sydney Morning Herald*, 15 November.

Doern, B. and R. Johnson 2006, *Rules, Rules, Rules, Rules: Multi-Level Regulatory Governance*, University of Toronto Press, Toronto.

Doern, B. 2003, 'Improving regulatory relations in multi-level governance: Principles and mechanisms', paper presented to the Expert Meeting on Regulatory Cooperation Between Levels of Governments, Organisation for Economic Cooperation and Development, Paris.

Jordana, J. and D. Levi-Faur 2004, 'The politics of regulation in the age of governance', in J Jordana and D Levi-Faur, (eds) *The Politics of Regulation. Institutions and regulatory reforms for the age of governance*, Edward Elgar, Cheltenham, UK, pp. 1-28.

Lynch, A. 2006, 'Time to reshape Australian federalism', *Sydney Morning Herald*, 15 November.

McConkey, M. and P. Dutil 2006, 'Dissecting Discourses of 21st Century Regulatory Governance', in M. McConkey and P. Dutil (eds), *New Directions: Dreaming of the Regulatory Village; Speaking of the Regulatory State*. No. 18, Institute of Public Administration Canada, Toronto, pp. 1-10.

NTC 2004, *Improving the Regulatory Framework for Rail Safety in Australia*, Discussion Paper, National Transport Commission, Melbourne.

NTC 2006, 'New National Rail Safety Laws: Implementation Program', *Information Bulletin*, July, National Transport Commission, Melbourne.

OECD 2002, *OECD Review of Regulatory Reform, Regulation Policies in OECD Countries. From intervention to regulatory governance*, Organisation for Economic Cooperation and Development, Paris.

Owens, H. 2003, 'Rail Reform Strategies: The Australian Experience', NBER Working Paper No. 9592, National Bureau of Economic Research, Cambridge, MA.

Painter, M. 1998, *Collaborative Federalism: Economic reform in Australia in the 1990s*, Cambridge University Press, Cambridge.

Patty, A. 2006, 'The push for national teacher standards', *Sydney Morning Herald*, 11 October, p. 7.

Productivity Commission 1999, *Progress in Rail Reform*, Report no. 6, AusInfo, Canberra.

Quiggin, J. 2006, 'Regulation. Benefits of Diversity', *Australian Policy Online*, February 2, 2006, viewed at 16 February 2006, www.apo.org.au

Regulation Taskforce 2006, 'Rethinking Regulation: Report of the Taskforce on Reducing Regulatory Burdens on Business', Report to the Prime Minister and the Treasurer, Canberra.

Steane, P. and P. Carroll 2001, 'Australia, the OECD and the Post-NPM World', in L. Jones, J. Guthrie and P. Steane (eds), *Learning from International Public Management Reform*, JAI, Elsevier Science Ltd, Amsterdam, pp. 29-44.

Stevenson, G. 1987, *Rail Transportation and Australian Federalism*, Research Monograph No. 48, Centre for Research on Federal Financial Relations, Australian National University, Canberra.

Twomey, A. and G. Withers 2007, 'Federalist Paper 1. Australia's Federal Future: Delivering Growth and Prosperity', A report for the Council for the Australian Federation, Sydney.

Wilson, T. and B. Moore 2006, 'Regulatory reform in land transport', paper to the Productivity Commission Roundtable, Productive Reform in a Federal System, National Transport Commission, Melbourne.

Chapter 5. The national reform agenda: origins and objectives

Helen Silver[1]

Introduction

The aim of this chapter is to examine the origins and the objectives of the National Reform Agenda. The Council of Australian Government's (COAG) National Reform Agenda is an important reform initiative that is close to the heart of many public policy makers across Australia. The Victorian Government has been advocating since 2005, particularly through COAG, that all governments need to develop a new National Reform Agenda with regulatory reform and human capital at its heart.

Throughout 2006, officials from all jurisdictions worked hard to make the National Reform Agenda (NRA) a reality. As work advanced on this — whether through ongoing discussions with the Commonwealth and other jurisdictions, or through the development of specific reform proposals — state jurisdictions remained convinced of the potential and necessity of a new reform agenda. Arguing for change has not been easy but there is strong evidence that supports the case for this reform proposal.

The chapter will cover the rationale for this agenda, outlining the evidence that has compelled policy makers and public servants to persevere. 'Evidence-based' policy has been a key tool in contemplating and developing the argument for a new reform approach. The chapter will then examine what the National Reform Agenda, including regulation and human capital reform, should look like and, finally, discuss the critical success factors for genuine national reform. It is important to note that, as this is a reform agenda that continues to evolve, the paper only covers the period to November 2006 and does not consider important developments that have occurred since that time.

The impact and legacy of past reforms

Since 2005 the Council of Australian Governments has become a critical forum where a strong debate around a new National Reform Agenda has occurred. The Victorian Government, with support from the other states, has played a leadership role in this debate, consistently arguing at COAG and in COAG related fora that behind Australia's current prosperity is a legacy of reform by previous governments. The Victorian Government has also argued that more needs to be done. The first wave of reform from the early 1980s saw the floating of the dollar, the deregulation of financial markets and the effective end of tariff barriers designed to protect Australia's industries.

The second wave of reform from the early to mid 1990s included agreement to implement National Competition Policy (NCP) as its centrepiece. Australia has enjoyed some 15 consecutive years of economic growth and these two major waves of economic reform are behind what has been described as 'the miracle economy' (The Economist 2003). Supporters of the NRA have argued that, while we should recognise our achievements to date, the evidence suggests there is no time for complacency and more reforms are required.

The evidence that supports new reforms

Evidence of the need for continuing reform is compelling. Australia has enjoyed unprecedented prosperity in recent decades. We are experiencing the longest period of continuous economic growth since Federation, which is manifest in the steady increase in productivity and the steady decrease in unemployment. However, despite our recent successes, in 2004 Australia still ranked in the bottom 10 countries of the OECD in terms of labour productivity.

In addition, we also know that labour force participation rates of Australian men and women are generally lower than in the United States and the OECD average. There is significant room to improve our workforce participation rates for women with dependent children and for the older age cohorts. Supporters of the NRA have argued that we need to get better at assisting to women combine work and family and enabling older age groups to phase into retirement. A strong argument in the NRA arena has been that governments must look ahead and plan for the future.

Surveys of the global economic landscape by organisations such as the OECD reveal other major challenges facing Australia in the medium to long term. These challenges are well recognised by all Australian governments, commentators and the OECD (OECD 2006). In putting forward the case for the NRA, the Victorian Government has argued that the new set of challenges facing Australia over the coming decades are particularly linked to the ageing population and a more competitive international environment.

We know that our ageing population will present governments with considerable economic and fiscal pressures, particularly on the health system. In the next 40 years, around 45% of our population will not be participating in the workforce. This will place an enormous burden on those still in the workforce. At the same time, business will continue to depend on recruiting an efficient, skilled and healthy workforce.

We are also aware of the increasing impact of international competitive pressures and related opportunities. In coming decades China will overtake the United States as the world's largest economy and, with India, will make up the top three. This will place pressure on both low wage and high wage jobs and industries. These economic changes will make skills increasingly important.

NRA policy makers have argued that preparing our workforce for the future will be a challenge for all governments and that the challenges ahead in the coming decades demand a reform agenda that is more ambitious than that of the 1980s and 1990s.

Data from the Groningen Growth and Development Centre (GGDC) in 2005 shows that Australia's ranking against other OECD countries, based on GDP per capita (USD in 2002), declined from the 1950s to the early 1980s but started to pick up in the early to mid 1990s, arguably coinciding with the first and second waves of reform. It has been argued that, in order for Australia to continue climbing the global income ladder, we need a new, ambitious agenda of national economic reform.

With considerable room for improvement in our current performance and the well recognised challenges of an ageing population and a more competitive international environment described above, there is a compelling argument for a new wave of reform. The argument has called for a third wave of reform which builds on and leverages our current successes so that we are well positioned to continue 'punching above our weight' on the global stage.

The third wave of reform explained

In response to what Australian state governments considered as inadequate reform at the national level, coinciding with an understanding of the clear need to address the future challenges, the Victorian Government has argued for (and indeed COAG has accepted) three key components under the new NRA. These components are competition, regulation and human capital. In essence, competition is about more competitive markets, regulation is about reducing red tape and human capital is about a healthier, better skilled and a more motivated workforce.

From 2005, the Victorian Government actively argued at COAG that a clear vision for the next decade was needed, with all governments needing to work together to boost Australia's economic productivity and workforce participation. The evidence suggests and COAG has agreed, that this can be done by boosting productivity and lifting participation through a continued focus on business (through the lenses of competition and regulation mentioned above) and a new focus on human capital.

The NRA is a complex, interrelated and long term agenda with a simple message at its heart. It argues that governments need to work together for the common good to drive improvements to our productivity and lift workforce participation. The Victorian Government has also argued that the NRA requires a decade-long focus on reform in order to gain more immediate opportunities, such as completing the NCP reforms and extending the NCP reform agenda to include regulatory and infrastructure reform.

Completing competition reforms and further reducing the regulatory burden

The Victorian Government has argued that significant gains can be made through completing the competition reforms started in the 1990s and reducing regulatory burden. It also argued that the proposed new 'human capital' agenda offers the biggest economic potential and that additional reform opportunities should look at new reform initiatives linked to increasing the productive capacity of our people through health, education and training and work incentives. It has recognised the need to complete competition reform and also reduce the burden of regulation on our business. One line of argument pursued at COAG by supporters of the NRA has been that completing NCP and pursuing further regulation reform would allow Australia to drive further improvements to our already highly competitive and well functioning markets. While most NCP reforms have been substantially completed, there remains scope for further gains, including through further progress towards a fully integrated national electricity market, completing commitments to legislation review under NCP, improving infrastructure regulation and competitive neutral road and rail pricing.

Another significant opportunity for governments is to reduce the burden of red tape on our businesses. The 'regulatory burden' can be improved through addressing both the process (via gate-keeping arrangements) and outcomes (via targets that can be objectively verified). The Victorian Government has led by example in this area. In July 2006 it announced, in addition to COAG initiatives, that there would be no new regulatory burden with its introduction of an 'offsetting simplification' for new regulations — effectively the identification of a 'one in, one out' principle with regard to regulation. The Victorian Government also committed at that time to reducing the current burden by committing to a target of a 15% reduction in the cost of administrative burdens in three years and 25% in five years.

In 2006, progress was made at the national level on reducing the regulatory burden. The COAG Communiqué of February 2006 notes that COAG has agreed 'to a range of measures to ensure best-practice regulation-making and review and to make 'down payment' on regulatory reduction by taking action now to reduce specific regulation 'hotspots' (COAG 2006).

Following the February 2006 decision, jurisdictions have been working together on a range of issues. This includes best practice regulation-making within jurisdictions through improved gate keeping processes and across jurisdictions through developing principles for determining when uniform, harmonised or jurisdiction-specific regulation is 'best'.

COAG also agreed to take action with regard to 10 'hotspots' at its February and July 2006 meetings, that is, priority areas where regulatory overlap is seen as impeding economic activity. The hotspots include: Occupational Health and Safety (OHS); Building Regulation; Rail Safety Regulation; Environmental Assessments & Approvals; and Business Registration Processes. The rationale was that if governments could make real progress in these areas, they could demonstrate the potential for further reform. Many of these areas, such as OHS, are affirmed as a priority focus by the publicly expressed views of business interests, notably the Business Council of Australia. Jurisdictions have also been working together on a framework for the annual review of existing regulation in each jurisdiction for the purposes of reducing the burden on business. The Victorian Government has demonstrated a commitment to this agenda with the establishment of a standalone gatekeeper in relation to regulation — the Victorian Competition and Efficiency Commission (VCEC) — and with its 'Reducing the Regulatory Burden' initiative that includes the ambitious targets for reducing the regulatory compliance burden of 15 % over 3 years and 25 % over the next five years (Department of Treasury and Finance (Victoria) 2006).

The human capital agenda

The human capital agenda mentioned above is a particularly innovative and compelling component in the 'story' about the need for reform. The Human Capital agenda argues that Australia needs a healthier, skilled, more motivated workforce so that our businesses can continue to compete and succeed in the global economy. We know that, in addition to the well-founded social reasons, there are strong economic reasons why governments should invest in improving people's health outcomes, improving the skills of our population and creating a motivated workforce.

The argument about the importance of Australia's human capital is at the heart of the NRA. The NRA approach at COAG is a marked change from a time in the past when governments came together at COAG to discuss social policy reforms which tended to focus in isolation on the 'latest crisis'. For example, the previous premiers' conferences focused on isolated policy content such as the number of hospital beds, 'drugs' in schools at COAG in 1999 and child protection at COAG in 2002. The NRA has tried to move away from 'crisis management' by encouraging a view across portfolios — looking for synergies in education outcomes and health outcomes. Promoting healthy living in schools is an obvious example. The NRA puts forward a long-term perspective, looking at government interventions across a lifecycle, for example from developing good diet and exercise habits in childhood to maintaining good habits as we get older and managing good health in the longer term.

This long-term perspective is particularly important. The NRA allows governments to make specific decisions about investing in early intervention based on the evidence that this investment is critical if we are to make a difference to long-term outcomes. The NRA provides governments with a framework that promotes a long term view.

How big could the gains be?

Modelling by the Victorian Department of Treasury has estimated that the benefits from reform are significant and will continue to grow for 20 years (Department of Treasury and Finance (Vic) 2005). They show that NRA's potential economic significance could add some 3% to 5% to annual GDP after 10 years, with more than a 10% increase after 25 years. This would amount to an additional $65 billion to the Australian economy. The preliminary estimates from the Federal Government's Productivity Commission confirm Victoria's conclusion that the potential economic benefits from human capital reform are particularly significant and warrant a concerted effort from policy makers and political leaders (Productivity Commission 2006). One example of an area where reforms could lead to significant gains is by lowering rates of diabetes, an area which is part of the first tranche of specific human capital reforms that COAG agreed to consider in 2007. Further, the Victorian Department of Treasury's modelling of specific diabetes initiatives demonstrates that the vast bulk of these financial benefits will flow to the Commonwealth (as increased income tax and reduced calls on health spending and welfare payments). These outcomes raise the question of funding for these actions and the equitable sharing of the benefits of reform.

COAG's commitment to the NRA

In 2006, building on discussions that took place in 2005, COAG reached significant agreements on the NRA. In February it agreed to, among other issues: endorse the NRA; an overall framework of multilateral and jurisdictional-specific policy proposals; the creation of a COAG Reform Council (CRC); and to a fair sharing of costs and benefits (COAG 2006a). In July 2006, among other agreements there was: a re-affirmation of a 10 year NRA framework and a fair sharing of costs and benefits; agreement to 11, indicative high-level human capital outcomes; that the COAG Reform Council would assess costs and benefits; agreement to an initial focus on three human capital areas, as a first step, by the next COAG meeting; and agreement that the next COAG, to be held in early 2007, would consider specific reform proposals being developed by the Human Capital Working Group and Competition and Regulation Working Group (and their subgroups) with representatives from all jurisdictions (COAG 2006b).

Factors to ensure the success of the third wave

A number of factors underpin the success of the NRA, which brings together a number of related objectives. These objectives primarily include economic prosperity, social cohesion and healthy federalism.

First, the NRA has economic prosperity as a key objective, through improving productivity and participation and by being able to meet the new economic challenges of an ageing population, international competitive challenges and an increasing premium on skills in the economy.

Another objective is social cohesion, thereby enabling the best outcomes for the individual and by improving social cohesion more generally. The NRA has argued for the benefits and necessity, of promoting social inclusion and mobility, through a lens of economic reform. The joint goals of participation and productivity link closely to the proposed human capital agenda in terms of the need to improve literacy and numeracy at school; more successful youth transitions; raising adult skills; and improving workforce participation by preventing illness and disease.

Finally, NRA has building a healthy federalism as an objective. Public policy makers in Victoria have argued that, through establishing a framework that creates the right incentives for all governments to work together towards common outcomes, the NRA can improve the health of the Australian federal system. The NRA has challenged governments to change the way they work together, to focus on agreed outcomes rather than contestable 'inputs' and 'outputs' and to focus on a truly fair sharing of the costs and benefits.

COAG has agreed on the solid conceptual framework for the National Reform Agenda. That is, having agreed the vision, objectives and reform priorities, governments agreed to focus on outcomes and measuring progress against those outcomes. This is a significant shift from the 'old' ways of COAG, where there was an undue emphasis on specific inputs and actions. The 'old' way of doing things had fostered an unproductive game of 'points scoring' and 'blame shifting' and resulted in a financial framework between governments (for example, specific purpose payments), that could be too focused on administration and red tape and too little on outcomes. By agreeing on what governments want to achieve and how they will measure progress towards that achievement, the debate moved away from 'who does what and for how much' towards 'what we need to do and for what benefit'.

A new way of states working with the Commonwealth

The NRA proposed a new way of working with the Commonwealth that included four key elements: collaboration; an outcomes-based approach; jurisdictional flexibility; and a long-term and integrated reform agenda across portfolio areas. The Victorian Government has argued that collaboration is about agreeing to implement policies in more integrated ways, including collaboration on interface issues. An outcomes-based approach is about focusing policies on achieving outcomes for the community, not prescribing actions. Jurisdictional flexibility relies on moving away from a one-size-fits-all approach to reform that allows jurisdictions to pursue outcomes in ways that reflect different systems, circumstances and priorities. Finally, the Victorian Government has argued that the NRA is about a long-term and integrated reform agenda across portfolio areas where COAG would focus on the outcomes that matter to the economy and community and collectively undertake long-term integrated reform across portfolio areas.

We are not starting on a green field site. Australia has successfully implemented collaborative national reform previously. The NCP is widely acknowledged as one of the most successful collaborative reform efforts since Federation. The Productivity Commission's review of National Competition Policy reforms identified four key success factors that made NCP so successful (Productivity Commission 2005). These were: recognition by all governments of the need for reform; broad agreement on the priority problem areas; a solid conceptual framework and information base to guide policy prescriptions; and some highly effective procedural and institutional mechanisms to implement reform.

The NCP procedural and institutional mechanisms were important and included transparent and independent monitoring of progress and outcomes, robust accountability arrangements and financial incentives to states and territories. Gary Banks, the chair of the Productivity Commission has proposed that the framework to drive successful reform into the twenty-first century should contain 'independent monitoring and assessment of progress in implementing agreed reforms', 'robust accountability arrangements (including) progress measures'; and 'financial incentives to the states and territories to enable an appropriate sharing of the costs and benefits of reform' (Banks 2006).

These are all elements which the Victorian Government has advocated as critical to the success of the NRA. The evidence suggests that without the appropriate incentives and a robust framework, governments will not be able to deliver the ambitious reform agenda required to meet the challenges ahead.

The importance of the right institutional arrangements

Ensuring that the right institutional arrangements exist to provide the right incentives to deliver against agreed outcomes is the critical success factor for the NRA. Having an effective independent body to monitor the reform agenda is part of this. COAG in July 2006 went some way towards achieving this, in agreeing to establish the COAG Reform Council (CRC). The Productivity Commission has also recognised the importance of incentives. Gary Banks, Chairman of the Productivity Commission in a 2006 speech to the 'Making the

Boom Pay' conference in Melbourne succinctly described this issue in the context of regulation:

> While many regulatory reforms will be clearly beneficial to the jurisdictions implementing them, reforms directed at achieving national consistency may not yield benefits to individual jurisdictions commensurate with national gains. In such circumstances, there may be a case for the Australian Government to provide financial incentives for jurisdictions to take a broader view.[2]

The case is even more stark in the area of human capital reform, where the States and Territories will do the bulk of the 'heavy lifting'. Modelling suggests that the Commonwealth will receive the majority of the benefits. While COAG has agreed in principle to the fair sharing of the costs and benefits of reform, it remains to be seen how this agreement will be implemented.

Early support

This case for the need for a third wave of reform has been supported by key stakeholders like the International Monetary Fund (IMF) and the Business Council of Australia, who have argued strongly for a new wave of national reform. At the meeting of the IMF Executive Board in October 2006, directors 'welcomed the agreement between the Australian and state governments on the ambitious NRA to lift productivity and labour participation over the next decade' (International Monetary Fund 2006). The Productivity Commission *Annual Report* in October 2006 noted that:

> The NRA is wide-ranging and ambitious. It lays down some challenging objectives for reform within its 'human capital' stream, along with more specific initiatives in the competition and regulatory reform streams to complete and build on the NCP.[3]

As these quotes indicate, support for the NRA is strong among and widespread. There is explicit recognition that Australia must undertake ambitious reforms and that incentives serve as the best way to drive this process. There is also a sense that reform commitments, particularly in relation to competition and regulation reform, need to be put into action quickly.

Conclusion

We are at an interesting point in the history of our Federation. There are pressures on our federal system through the changing expectations of the Australian population, the evolving legal landscape and the increasing pressure on governments to deliver 'more for less'. If implemented completely, the National Reform Agenda offers governments a way to respond to these pressures and creates a framework for a decade of collaborative national reform. It also can provide us with the opportunity to equip Australians with better skills, better health and better systems to respond to the economic demands of the future.

References

Banks, G. 2006, *Regulation for Australia's Federation in the 21st Century*, Chairman, Productivity Commission, 3 November.

COAG 2006a, *Communiqué,* Council of Australian Government Meeting, 10 February 2006, Page 9, at http://www.coag.gov.au/meetings/100206/coag100206.pdf

COAG 2006b, *Communiqué,* Council of Australian Government Meeting, 14 July 2006 as at http://www.coag.gov.au/meetings/140706/docs/coag140706.pdf

Department of Treasury and Finance 2005, 'Rewards from Reform: Higher Productivity and Labour Participation', August.

Department of Treasury and Finance 2006, 'Reducing the Regulatory Burden: The Victorian Government's Plan to reduce red tape'.

Groningen Growth and Development Centre 2005, 'Total Economy Database', *Public Information Notice (PIN) No. 06/123*, International Monetary Fund 2006. page 3, October 23, at http://www.imf.org/external/pubs/ft/scr/2006/cr06374.pdf

OECD 2006, 'Economic Surveys: Australia Volume 2006/12', July.

Productivity Commission 2005, *Review of National Competition Policy Reforms*, Report No. 33, Canberra.

Productivity Commission 2006a, *Annual Report 2005-06*, page 9, Productivity Commission, Canberra at http://www.pc.gov.au/research/annrpt/annualreport0506/annualreport0506.pdf

Productivity Commission 2006b. *Potential Benefits of the National Reform Agenda*, Report to the Council of Australian Governments, Canberra.

The Economist 2003,'The Lucky Country: Is Australia's economic miracle sustainable?' in *The Economist*, 6th March. http://www.econ.jku.at/Boeheim/teaching/economist/Australian%20Miracle.htm

ENDNOTES

[1] I would like to acknowledge the assistance of Elizabeth Langdon in completing this chapter.

[2] Gary Banks, 'Regulation for Australia's Federation in the 21st Century'. Paper presented at the Melbourne Institute Conference *Making the Boom Pay: Securing the Next Generation of Prosperity*, 2–3 November 2006. Accessed 20 May 2008 at: http://www.melbourneinstitute.com/conf2006/pdffiles/Session%205/Gary%20Banks_paper.pdf

[3] Productivity Commission 2006a. Annual Report 2005-06, page 9, Productivity Commission, Canberra at http://www.pc.gov.au/research/annrpt/annualreport0506/annualreport0506.pdf

Chapter 6. Rethinking Regulation

Peter Carroll

Introduction

The aim of this chapter is to assess the *Report of the Commonwealth Government's Taskforce on Reducing the Regulatory Burden on Business* (the *Banks Report*), released in April 2006 and the government's endorsement of those recommendations (Australian Government 2006a; 2006b). The endorsement, followed by the beginning of the implementation of the recommendations, constitutes, together with the items encompassed in the National Reform Agenda, a centrepiece of the third wave of regulatory reform in Australia. The focus of the chapter is the report's recommendations with regard to the system for making regulation with regard to business, particularly the regulation impact statement process (RIS), as discussed in chapter two. In summary, the overall assessment is that there is much in the report to be commended but that it is, for the most part, one that calls for greater commitment and support for existing systems for making and implementing business regulation, rather than a fundamental rethinking of the existing system.

The *Banks Report*: origins

The origins of the Commonwealth Government's 2005 decision to establish the Taskforce on Reducing the Regulatory Burden on Business can be found in the long-standing commitment of successive Australian Governments to a minimum of effective business regulation as a primary means of ensuring the international competitiveness of the Australian economy, combined with pressure from peak business associations such as the Australian Chamber of Commerce and Industry (ACCI), the Business Council of Australia (BCA) and from the Productivity Commission, part of whose role is to provide advice in relation to the regulation of business (see, for example, Howard 1997; ACCI 2005a;2005b; BCA 2005a; 2005b; Productivity Commission 2003; 2004; 2005; Banks 2003a; 2003b; 2004). The Taskforce was designed primarily to identify the views of business, for the benefit of business and with its members being drawn from business (Australian Government 2006a: A1). The Taskforce's Report was submitted on 31 January 2006 and released, together with the government's Interim Response to its recommendations, on 7 April (Banks 2006; Australian Government 2006).

The core arguments of the *Banks Report*

The Report's core arguments for reform are contained in the first three chapters. In summary, chapter one sets the scene by noting that all societies need an appropriate level of regulation, that there have been substantial gains from regulatory reform over the past 20 years but, also, that there has been a rapid increase in both the volume of regulation, some justified, some not, with rising concern from business as to the increasing cost of compliance, leading to the need for a new wave of reform. Chapter two of the report expands on the basic arguments put forward in chapter one, stressing, in addition, that, while much of the new regulation might be appropriate, some was not and, importantly, that it was the cumulative burden of regulation on individual businesses that was of especial concern, leading to increasing compliance costs and the displacement of time and resources that otherwise could be spent on more creative and innovative behaviour (Banks 2006: 5). It then puts forward the core of its argument in favour of reform, indicating that the fundamental cause of increasing regulation is 'increasing risk aversion in many spheres of life' (Banks 2006: 14). In turn, the report argues, while an effective regulation-making and administrative system should 'mediate', the impact of the increasing demands that arise from an increasingly risk averse society, this was not happening for four basic reasons (Banks 2006: 15):

- the real costs of regulation are 'hidden', from view as they are the 'off-budget', costs of business and society compliance with regulation;
- the cumulative cost of regulation is not often considered as most departments and agencies have responsibility only for specific regulation and little concern for its cumulative nature;
- the culture of some regulators fosters excessive and poor regulation as they respond to incentives to 'protect' consumers with heavy handed, prescriptive, legalistic enforcement, a 'government knows best' attitude and a general distrust of business people; and
- the regulation impact statement (RIS) system — introduced to minimise the externalities noted above — helped, but, the report notes, was often circumvented or treated as an afterthought.

The report underlines a pressing need for regulatory reform encompassing the reform of specific regulations, regulation-making and implementation processes. In addition, the report places special emphasis on reducing the compliance burden (Banks 2006: 15-16). The reform imperative, says the report, is heightened by the challenges posed by the following:

- an ageing society;
- increased competition from low-cost and lightly-regulated industries in China and India;
- the inherent limitations of small scale operations in a small economy;
- substantial distances between domestic and international markets; and
- the increasing rate of regulatory reform taking place in other countries such as the UK and the USA (Banks 2006: 16).

While the government's responses to the report do not formally and explicitly indicate its agreement with its analysis of the underlying causes of regulation, the fact that it commended the Taskforce on its work and, at least in relation to those recommendations related to the making and implementation of regulation, accepted all bar two of its 29 recommendations, suggests that it was sympathetic to that analysis.

The risk-averse society proposition is contentious, similar to that expressed by UK Prime Minister, Tony Blair, with regard to British society (Banks 2005: 4; 2006a: 14). Whatever strength it has is markedly lessened by the following three flaws. The first is the report's failure to explain adequately how an increasingly risk-averse society could have tolerated the major microeconomic reforms in the later 1980s, 1990s and the earlier part of the 2000s — the same period in which social risk-averseness was allegedly growing (Banks 2006: i). This is not to deny that there may well have been a rise in the extent and type of regulation in recent decades, however, this is as likely to have arisen because of established, if variable, patterns of interest group pressure (including from business), as from a change in the risk tolerance of Australian society. The second flaw is the report's failure to produce any systematic, empirical evidence as to past and present trends in the 'risk averseness' of Australian society to support its argument. The third flaw is the somewhat circular nature of the risk averseness argument, with the cause of the increasing volume and poor quality of some regulation being identified as risk averseness and the only 'evidence' of risk averseness being the growth in volume of regulation measured, very crudely, by reference to the number of pages of legislation per annum.

The report does provide some fascinating statistics to illustrate and support its claim for the growth in volume of regulation, noting that the Australian Parliament had passed more pages of legislation since 1990 than it had in the first 90 years of federation (Banks 2006: 6). It notes that the growth in the number of pages does not necessarily indicate a similar, dramatic growth in regulations, however, the statistics clearly are meant to impress the reader and imply that there has been a similar, if not quite as dramatic growth in regulation. However, it could be convincingly argued that the spectacular growth in volume of regulation at the height of the microeconomic reform program in the 1990s was, in addition to the promulgation of new regulation, at least partly a result of attempts to render existing regulation into 'plain English' in order to make its intent clearer and more specific. The use of 'plain English', while important, does not bring with it any necessary reduction in the number of words needed to expound complex regulation.

The report also stresses that the compliance cost to business 'may well total billions of dollars' (Banks 2006:13). It provides estimates from various studies that indicate the total, annual cost is anywhere from $11 billion to $86 billion, indicating its preference for the more conservative estimates (Banks 2006: 14). However, the value of presenting such wildly differing estimates, other than to convince the less-informed reader of the cost of regulation, is highly questionable, especially given the view expressed in the report that none of the studies quoted estimate the net cost of regulation and that they should not be viewed as 'robust estimates' (Banks 2006: 13-14). This begs the question as to why they were included for they can hardly contribute to informed debate, given their wildly varying estimates.

The argument that the real costs of regulation are the hidden, off-budget costs of business and society compliance is similarly difficult to accept as a fundamental cause of over-regulation. If the costs were so well hidden, would it not have been far more difficult for business interests and the Productivity Commission (and its predecessors) to persuade successive governments of both political persuasions to undertake major waves of regulatory reform? Moreover, both directly and indirectly, the annual reports of the Commission have drawn attention to such costs. This is not to reject the fact that the full costs are not known with any degree of precision and that, if they were, governments might be more reluctant to impose regulation without fuller evaluation of those costs.

The argument that the cumulative cost of regulation is rarely considered as most departments and agencies have responsibility only for specific regulation and little concern for its cumulative nature, is a good, if not fully convincing point. However, in the shape of the Productivity Commission, it is an argument that has had a powerful, articulate and well-publicised proponent for many years, backed by business voices and, again, in the shape of successive waves of regulatory reform since the mid-1980s, has had some impact. Perhaps, an at least as important a cause has been the failure of the Commission and business to provide accurate and convincing data as to the net impact of business regulation to support the argument. This author, for example, has not been able to identify any convincing estimates of the typical, net cost to a small business and to society of the full range of regulation to which they are subject.

The argument that the culture of some regulators fosters excessive and poor regulation, however accurate as a portrayal of business views of regulators, lacks any firm basis in systematic research. Only if and when convincing, reliable data is provided should it be given any credence. This is not to deny that some individual regulators may have such attitudes and approaches, similar to attitudes and approaches displayed by some businesses toward some clients.

The final argument, in relation to the weaknesses of the RIS process and the associated systems for making and implementing regulation, is elaborated at greater length in chapter seven of the report and is discussed at length in the following sections.

Recommendation 7.1: six principles of good regulatory process and the RIS system

In recommending the adoption of six principles for the making and implementation of regulation, the Taskforce is doing little more than asking the government to re-endorse a system for the making of regulation in relation to business that it had endorsed since entering office — the RIS system. Why the Taskforce should be asking, in effect, for a re-endorsement of the basic principles underpinning the RIS system is explained by its ambiguous view of RIS. It identifies its weaknesses as a major factor contributing to the growth of regulation and its cost but also notes that it is '…sound in principle' but, unfortunately, that it had not been consistently applied, a barely veiled criticism of both the executive and administrative arms of government (Banks 2006: 15). There is no suggestion that RIS may *not* be 'sound in principle'. The business submissions to the report expressed strong support for the RIS system but also noted that it needed strengthening, a view that the Taskforce endorsed in recommendations 7.2, 7.3, 7.4, 7.8, 7.9, 7.10, 7.12, 7.13, that, in summary proposed: one, the standard of analysis considered acceptable for a regulation impact statement should be increased for the regulation in question to be approved; two, that it should be made harder for a regulatory proposal to proceed to a decision if the government's requirements for good process had not been adequately discharged; and three, that several basic elements of the system needed substantial strengthening (Banks 2006: vi).

While this author has a great deal of sympathy with the need for a rational, systematic approach to policy-making, whether it be with regard to business or any other area, the claim that RIS is sound in principle might be questioned, at least as regards its degree of 'fit' with the dynamics of politics in a democracy such as Australia's. In particular, it has to be remembered that any system for policy-making in a democracy will inevitably be subject to competing political forces — from those wishing change for the benefits they hope it will bring to those who resist change for fear the benefits that they currently receive will diminish or be eliminated. Policy-making — whether or not it is referred to as regulation-making — is an intensely political process, an arena in which regulation-making is determined as much by the relative power of the participants as by process and the quality of regulatory content. Efforts to promote a greater degree of rationality, such as the recommendations of the Taskforce in relation to RIS, are to be welcomed for the improvements in content and process performance they might bring but they are not immune from the exercise of power in the policy process. This is the central problem faced by those concerned at the growth of regulation and by RIS and its adherents. It is the reason that popularly elected ministers will always vary in their degree of support for such a system, for they are players in the policy process, acutely sensitive to its demands and constraints. If they are not they do not remain as ministers for any length of time. RIS may be sound in principle, if the principles involved are those derived from the assumptions that humans are perfectly rational in their motives and actions. Unfortunately, they are less sound when faced with the realities of a political system in which rationality is limited and motives often short-sighted and selfish.

Consulting with business: recommendations 7.5, 7.6, 7.7, 7.19, 7.20, 7.21, 7.22

The report expressed serious concern regarding inadequacies in consulting with business, noting, in particular, a survey undertaken by the Australian Public Service Commission that found that only 25% of regulatory agencies had engaged with the public when developing regulations (Australian Public Service Commission 2005: 56, as noted in Banks 2006: 152). Not unreasonably, it was felt that less than adequate consultation tended to result in poorer quality regulation and the report recommended that the government develop: in recommendation 7.5, a whole of government policy on consultation, with detailed principles to be followed by all departments and agencies; in recommendation 7.6, for major, proposed regulation, the preparation and release of an initial 'green chapter', to all relevant parties, followed by successive 'exposure', drafts to test out options with business interests; and in recommendation 7.7, a business consultation website that would automatically notify, on a voluntary basis, registered businesses and government agencies of new developments (Banks 2006: 154). All of these recommendations were accepted.

The authors of the report seem not to have appreciated the irony of calling for greater and more effective consultation with business at the same time as it was suggesting that existing consultation practices had partly resulted in too much inappropriate regulation in a risk-averse society. It seems to have been felt that business groups were perhaps not so risk-averse: that their more effective participation would lead to greater business influence and, hence, better quality and less regulation. While a cynic might feel otherwise, the call for more systematic consultation is appropriate, given the somewhat surprising lack of consultation, provided that safeguards are built in to the system to ensure that those being consulted do not 'capture', the regulators to the extent that their views become those embodied, untested, in regulation. In part to provide such a safeguard, the report recommended the establishment of standing consultative bodies consisting of stakeholder representatives for each regulation with a major impact on business and the development of a consultation code of conduct modelled on the UK's new system (Australian Government 2006a: 165).

Increasing analytical capacity: recommendations 7.2, 7.3, 7.4, 7.13

The lack of analytical capacity and expertise, especially with regard to cost/benefit analysis and risk assessment, was identified as a major failing and recommendations 7.2, 7.3, 7.4 and 7.13 were aimed at its improvement. The Report argued that improvements in this area were one of three key areas where reform was most needed as part of a concerted effort to identify and contain the compliance costs to business of increasing regulation, especially for small business. Its concerns were those that had been voiced in several reports from the Productivity Commission (see Productivity Commission 2005: 26).

Hence, the recommendations to increase analytical capacity are to be welcomed and all were accepted, although a few points can be made in relation to them. Recommendation 7.2, to use cost benefit analysis (CBA), to compare different regulatory options could, perhaps, have gone a little further. What type and range of regulatory options, for example, should be subject to CBA? What constitutes 'adequate risk analysis', as recommended by the report and who is to judge what is adequate? If ORR (now the Office of Best Practice Regulation), is to have this function, then, even accepting the government's commitment to the bulk of the Taskforce's recommendations it is difficult to see how it will be able to prevent a determined minister and department proceeding with regulations deemed inadequate by the ORR.

Recommendation 7.13, that departments and agencies should ensure that their capacity to undertake good regulatory analysis is adequately resourced is yet another 'motherhood', assertion for, in principle, no government could object to it, nor did the Australian Government. However, no specific resource allocation is suggested and, apart from the relatively minor amounts for an improved website, it is unlikely to result in substantially greater allocations to policy-making units within other departments and agencies unless their ministers and, ultimately, cabinet, agree to increased allocations in the annual budgetary processes. At best, in accepting the recommendation a signal has been sent to departments that appropriate resourcing for regulatory analysis is a government priority, so that if they feel current resources are not adequate and make a reasonable case, they will get a sympathetic hearing in budget negotiations. Those who gain the support of the ORR for their claims for greater funding might be somewhat more successful, assuming that the ORR achieves the greater power suggested above.

Saying 'no', to inadequate regulatory proposals: recommendations 7.8, 7.9, 7.10, 7.12

The development of appropriate analytical capacity will not, in itself, prevent inadequate regulatory proposals being considered and accepted by decision-makers — including cabinet. These four recommendations are designed to minimise the chances of this occurring. Recommendation 7.8 specifies the grounds on which an RIS can be judged inadequate; 7.9 recommends that 'institutional barriers' be put in place to prevent an inadequate proposal proceeding to a decision-maker; 7.10 recommends that cabinet agree to a revised 'Guide to Regulation' containing strengthened requirements on departments and agencies making regulation; 7.12 recommends that ministerial responsibility for overseeing the government's regulatory processes and reform program be elevated to cabinet level, thereby adding political 'muscle', to support rigour in the RIS process.

The emphasis on the use of relevant international standards in relation to the four recommendations is particularly interesting, with its stated presumption that their use in the domestic context is appropriate unless an adequate justification for a variation is provided in the RIS process. While the intent is clear — to reduce the costs to business of having to meet differing domestic and international standards — there are a number of potentially problematic issues such as:

- the presumption that existing, international standards are appropriate for the Australian context, unless proven otherwise, although regulators will have the opportunity of identifying their weaknesses;
- the increased attention that domestic regulators and business interests will have to give to the international institutions responsible for developing international standards if they are to participate effectively in the international decision-making processes involved;
- in a very real sense the locus of several, current, domestically focused decision processes will move to the international arena, requiring regulators to develop a thorough knowledge and expertise in operating in such arenas; and
- in turn, the accountability of the international institutions will have to be examined and assessed for adequacy otherwise a distinct threat to domestic democratic participatory processes might arise.

The unqualified acceptance of recommendation 7.9 is surprising because, on first reading, it suggests that the cabinet, ministers and relevant statutory authorities with regulation-making power will in future amend or even withdraw their proposed regulations following the decisions of public servants in the ORR regarding their compliance — or lack of it — with RIS requirements and the adequacy of their RIS. A second reading of the government's response corrects this impression, for the institutional arrangements are not made explicit and they will not necessarily involve the ORR — although it is difficult to see how the ORR will not be involved, given the expansion of its management and evaluation roles with regard to the RIS system. Moreover, in 'exceptional circumstances', regulatory proposals can still proceed to cabinet or other decision-makers for final, pre-parliamentary decision and the recommendation is restricted to regulatory proposals with undefined 'material business impacts'. Nevertheless, any new institutional arrangements that emerge will be of considerable interest for all those interested in government, for they may result in some form of self-denying ordinance that will restrict the capacity of ministers to submit regulatory proposals to cabinet and the associated capacity of regulators to submit, at an earlier stage in the process, regulatory proposals to their superiors.

Recommendation 7.12, that ministerial responsibility for overseeing the government's regulatory processes and reform program should be elevated to cabinet level was perhaps not well put, for ministerial responsibility for overseeing regulatory processes and reform programs ultimately does rest with cabinet. Therefore, the recommendation, as phrased, is redundant. What the Taskforce seems to have been recommending was that greater political support and commitment should be provided for the RIS process in general and, in particular, the ORR's judgements as to the adequacy of regulatory proposals that it scrutinises. At present, the minister responsible for the RIS process is a not a cabinet minister, although situated in the Treasury portfolio. While this provides somewhat more political muscle for the process than when RIS was first introduced, a minister with cabinet rank might be a more powerful advocate for RIS in speaking out against inadequate submissions in the cabinet room.

While the Taskforce's recommendation for the responsible minister to be of cabinet rank is understandable, all ministers are in a difficult situation with regard to processes such as RIS. In essence, they face a conflict of interest situation, on the one hand committed under the doctrine of collective cabinet responsibility to support cabinet's formal support for RIS but, on the other hand, as ministers responsible for departments, they face the prospect of a failed regulatory proposal if the RIS evaluation for proposals arising from their departments is negative. Moreover, the staff of ministerial offices and the heads of department and senior public servants are well aware of this situation. Whatever their personal feelings on the matter, it would be a very brave person who resisted the wishes of a minister by advising that a favoured regulation was not to be recommended and pursued following an adverse RIS assessment from the ORR.

In this context, if a cabinet minister was to have responsibility, for example, for arguing that a regulatory proposal should not be accepted for submission to cabinet on the grounds of an adverse RIS evaluation, that minister would be in a very difficult position. The minister whose department's submission was in question would undoubtedly resist, resulting in a conflict situation that would substantially increase tension in cabinet. Moreover, cabinet deliberations are not concerned only with the economic merits of regulatory proposals but with their political feasibility, a factor not incorporated in the RIS process or evaluations.

Measuring regulatory performance: recommendations 7.16, 7.17, 7.18, 7.27, 7.28, 7.29

In accepting recommendation 7.16, for the development of a wider range of performance indicators for annual reporting, a much needed step — and a brave one — has been taken for, assuming that a useful set of performance indicators are developed and put in place, they will enable more accurate judgements of performance by the Opposition, the media and the electorate. There is little doubt that the existing set of regulatory performance indicators, managed by the Office of Small Business, have had little or no impact. No department or agency seems to be using them, at least explicitly and in published sources, as a means of identifying the causes of poor performance, or for improving on existing performance, a situation of which the Office of Small Business and the ORR are well aware.

However, the task of developing a useful and effective set of indicators is going to be difficult. In essence, for example, most regulations are akin to theories, requiring that their targets either engage or not engage in defined sets of behaviours. At best, as with all theory in the social sciences, regulatory theory will be only partially successful in achieving its goals, depending upon the adequacy of theory itself, the efficiency with which it is implemented, the degree of compliance of the target group and the context within which it is implemented remaining relatively unchanging. To design a useful set of indicators in these circumstances will be a challenge, for it is likely that they will have to cover not only regulatory outcomes (in other words, 'did the regulation achieve its purpose?') — perhaps the indicator of most use for the executive — but also indicators for outputs and implementation.

In the interests of justice and equity, the acceptance of recommendation 7.17, for the establishment of mechanisms for internally reviewing decisions where they do not exist, seems to have been accompanied by a degree of reluctance, for it is an acceptance only in principle to *request* — not *require* — regulators to 'consider', internal review mechanisms, where appropriate. It is difficult to understand this apparent reluctance, other than on grounds of possible costs for, as the Taskforce asserts, effective appeal mechanisms help ensure fairness for those adversely impacted by a decision as well as providing potentially useful feedback to regulators as to inadequate regulation and inadequate implementation. In many cases, for example, existing appeal mechanisms could be used, such as the Administrative Review Tribunal, by simply extending their coverage. A similar degree of reluctance may be apparent in 7.18, where there is only agreement in principle to the recommendation that there should be provision for merit review of any administrative decision that can significantly affect the interests of individuals or enterprises. The Government notes that it will 'continue to scrutinise legislative proposals on a case-by-case basis', neatly side-stepping the fact that legislative proposals are not 'administrative decisions'. Hence, if this response is not simply careless drafting, the government has agreed only to examine new legislative proposals to ensure that, consistent with ARC guidelines, administrative decisions made under the legislative proposals are subject to appropriate merits review — which means that those presently existing are excluded. Yet, it can be presumed that the Taskforce made its recommendation, primarily, on the basis of a study of existing legislation and related administrative decisions. In effect, while not making it clear, the government seems to be rejecting the bulk of the intent of the recommendation.

Recommendations 7.27 and 7.28 are intended to ensure that all regulations are subject to review every five years, unless otherwise specified and, for those that 'escape' the RIS system or whose compliance costs are uncertain, they are to be subject to a review no later than two years after implementation. Both recommendations were accepted by the government. However, in what seems to be recognition by the Taskforce of the cost of such reviews, it recommended they take place 'following a screening process', 'with the scope of the review tailored to the nature of the regulation and its perceived performance.' While the realism of this recommendation can be appreciated, it does tend to contradict the intent of the six principles of regulation contained in recommendation 7.1, with its proposal for rigorous assessment of the need for any regulation, whether existing or new. Also, what is meant by a 'screening process', in recommendation 7.27, regarding the review of regulation that escapes the RIS system or whose compliance costs were uncertain? Its obvious meaning is that the result of the screening process will be that some regulation will not be reviewed in the two year period, presumably because it is performing appropriately and a review is, thus, not necessary. However, it has to be asked if it is possible to come to such a judgement merely through a 'screening' process. Why is not all regulation subject to such a screening process, rather than the more costly and time-consuming RIS process? Also, the lack of any specification as to what screening actually will involve does leave a great deal of discretion in the hands of the government of the day to determine the rigour of that process, a loop-hole that is sure to be taken advantage of by governments when pressing circumstances arise.

Review programs, harmonisation and regulatory competition: recommendations 7.24, 7.25

Recommendation 7.24 is that the Council of Australian Governments (COAG), should consider establishing a series of reviews targeted at areas where there is significant overlap and/or inconsistency between the Australian Government and state and territory government regulations. In agreeing to the recommendation, the government noted that COAG had already established such a review program. The COAG program continues the review of all relevant federal and state legislation with regard to business that was conducted under the National Competition Agreement in the 1996-2005 period, albeit on a smaller scale and focused on areas of unnecessary overlap and inconsistency and not primarily focused on anti-competitive elements. It recognises, if not explicitly, some of the limitations of some of the legislative reviews conducted under that agreement, as well as the continuing need to ensure that new, inadequate regulation is as far as possible, restrained. However, unlike the reviews considered under the agreement process, where all relevant legislation was reviewed, the reviews referred to in the COAG agreements will be at the discretion of each jurisdiction. This will enable governments to be selective in their choice of legislation for review, perhaps, in some cases, avoiding politically sensitive, but economically important, legislation. However, the fact that all Australian state and federal governments have agreed to the principles involved should enable substantial peer group pressure to be exerted on recalcitrant governments, in a manner somewhat akin to the OECD's peer review mechanism (see OECD 2003, for example).

Recommendation 7.25 — or an overarching institutional framework for the national harmonisation of regulation — has been accepted by Australian jurisdictions, noting progress in that regard in the context of COAG. However, the basic question of harmonisation in a federal system needs some more detailed consideration than that provided in the report. A requirement to examine ways of increasing harmonisation within existing regulatory frameworks was part of the brief given to the Taskforce (pA1 and p28) and several recommendations for harmonisation were made, both in relation to specific regulatory systems (for example, medical devices, 4.18, 4.27, consumer health and safety 4.44, conveyancing laws 4.63, tax 5.45 and in chapter seven, with regard to Australia-wide harmonisation, particularly recommendation 7.25). While the author does not dispute the value of appropriate harmonisation, it is of concern that the benefits of regulatory competition between jurisdictions in a federal system may be neglected, for a now voluminous literature indicates that regulatory competition can have substantial benefits. At best, however, the possible benefits of regulatory competition are referred to only indirectly in the report and the government's response, such as with regard to 7.25, where it notes that failsafe mechanisms should be put in place 'to ensure that any jurisdictional variations from national regulations are either legitimated by all parties or annulled', which implies that variations that are more efficient can be legitimated, if credible. However, the general tone of the recommendation and, indeed, of the Taskforce report, is that regulatory variation is for the most part unfortunate and unduly costly for business. Competition does have its costs, such as those imposed by the need to adjust products and services in order to satisfy regulatory variation between jurisdictions but, given its well-founded if not absolute acceptability in promoting economic efficiency, it is surprising that it did not achieve more attention in the regulatory context. A world of harmonised regulation is not necessarily efficient.

Conclusion

In conclusion, the Taskforce report provides a useful insight into the systems for making business regulation. However, several of its arguments, especially those relating to the alleged risk averseness of Australian society, are not convincing, at least without further refinement and more reliable data. In part, this may have been caused by the limited time available for such an important project. It is more convincing when it comes to the assessment of the RIS system and its recommendations for its strengthening, no doubt drawing upon its chair's knowledge and experience in the Productivity Commission. The Government clearly found the Taskforce's assessment convincing and accepted the bulk of its recommendations — most of which constituted improvements to existing processes and techniques rather than fundamental changes — although these will be re-interpreted in ways that will not unduly constrain government prerogative.

As the tenor of the specific comments made in this chapter suggest, a large proportion of the recommendations made and accepted by the government represent a plea for more effective support and resourcing for a system that is already largely in place but that lacks the full extent of political and senior, administrative commitment and support needed to make it effective. Its positive reception suggests that commitment and support has now been increased, which should provide some reassurance to those in the Productivity Commission and business who have been expressing rising concern over the volume and quality of regulation. But, any government's capacity to provide support and commitment is limited and variable, swinging from issue area to issue area in line with changing socio-economic realities. The greatest value of the report might be that it made the pendulum swing in the direction of regulation and its improvement.

References

ACCI, 2005a, 'Holding Back the Red Tape Avalanche: A Regulatory Reform Agenda for Australia', Position Chapter, November.

— 2005b, Modern Workplace: Safer Workplace — An Australian Industry Blueprint for Improving Health and Safety, April.

Australian Government, 2006a, *Rethinking Regulation: Report of the Taskforce on Reducing Regulatory Burdens on Business Interim Response*, as at 28

June 2006, at http://www.pm.gov.au/news/media_releases/media_Release1869.html

Australian Government 2006b, 'Rethinking Regulation: Report of the Taskforce on Reducing Regulatory Burdens on Business Australian Government's Response', as at 20 November 2006, at http://www.eowa.gov.au/Reporting_And_Compliance/Australian_Government_Response.pdf

Australian Public Service Commission 2005, *State of the Service 2004-05*, Commonwealth of Australia, November.

Banks, G. 2003a, *Reducing the business costs of regulation*, March, Productivity Commission, as at 12 June 2006, at http://www.pc.gov.au/speeches/cs20030320/index.html

— 2003b, *The good, the bad and the ugly: economic perspectives on regulation in Australia*, 2 October, Productivity Commission, as at 12 June 2006, at http://www.pc.gov.au/speeches/cs20031002/index.html

— 2004, *NCP and beyond: an agenda for national reform*, 6 December, Productivity Commission, as at 12 June 2006, at http://www.pc.gov.au/speeches/cs20041206/index.html

— 2005, 'Regulation-making in Australia: Is it broke? How do we fix it?', A public lecture at the ANU as part of the Public Lecture Series of the Australian Centre of Regulatory Economics (ACORE) and the Faculty of Economics and Commerce, ANU, Canberra, 7 July. As at 7 February 2007, at http://www.pc.gov.au/speeches/cs20050707/index.html

— 2006, *Rethinking Regulation*, January, as at 12 June 2006, at http://www.regulationtaskforce.gov.au/index.html

BCA 2005a, *Locking in or Losing Prosperity — Australia's Choice*, Business Council of Australia, as at 12 June 2006, at http://www.bca.com.au/content.asp?newsID=99077

BCA, 2005b, *Business Regulation Action Plan For Future Prosperity*, Business Council of Australia, as at 28 June 2006, at http://www.bca.com.au/content.asp?newsID=99099

Bell, 1996, *Time for Business,* the Report of the Small Business Deregulation Task Force, as at 11 June 2006, at http://www.daf.gov.au/reports/time_for_business.pdf

CAI, 1980, *Government Regulation in Australia*, CAI.

Deighton-Smith, R. 2006. Personal communication with the author.

Head, B. and E. McCoy (eds) 1991. *Deregulation or Better Regulation?*, Macmillan, South Melbourne.

Howard, J. 1997. *More Time for Business*, statement by Prime Minister Howard, as at 11 June 2006, at http://www.industry.gov.au/content/itrinternet/cmscontent.cfm?ObjectID=25D8598E-CFE8-47EA-BC45A29D63948869

— 2006, *Government Response to the Report of the Taskforce on Reducing the Regulatory Burdens on Business*, as at 7 April 2006, at http://www.pm.gov.au/news/media_releases/media_Release1869.html

Industries Assistance Commission 1984, *Annual Report 1983-1984*, Industries Assistance Commission, AGPS.

— 1985, *Annual Report 1984-1985*, Industries Assistance Commission, AGPS.

Industry Commission 1996a, *Stock take of Progress in Microeconomic Reform*, Industry Commission, AGPS.

— 1996b, *Regulation and its Review: 1995-96*, Industry Commission, Canberra.

OECD, 1995, 'Recommendation on Improving the Quality of Government Regulation', OECD, Paris.

— 1997, 'The OECD Report on Regulatory Reform: Synthesis', OECD, Paris.

— 2001, 'Businesses' Views on Red Tape: Administrative and Regulatory Burdens on Small and Medium-Sized Enterprises', OECD, Paris.

— 2003, *Practical Modalities of Peer Review in a Multilateral Framework on Competition*, COM/DAFFE/TD(2002)82/FINAL, at 20 September 2006, at http://www.oecd.org/competition

— 2005, 'OECD Guiding Principles for Regulatory Quality and Performance', OECD, Paris.

Office of Regulation Review 1998, *A Guide to Regulation* (second edition), Productivity Commission.

Productivity Commission 1999, *Regulation and its Review 1998-999*, AusInfo, Canberra.

— 2003, *Regulation and its Review 2002-03*, Annual Report Series, Productivity Commission, Canberra.

— 2005, *Regulation and its Review 2004-05*, Annual Report Series, Productivity Commission, Canberra.

Self, P. 1977, 'Econocrats and the Policy Process: The Politics and Philosophy of Cost-Benefit Analysis', London, Macmillan, 1975.

Taskforce 2005, 'Taskforce Issues Chapter', as at 3 July 2006, at http://www.regulationtaskforce.gov.au/issueschapter/index.html

World Bank 2004, *Doing Business in 2005: Removing Obstacles to Growth*, World Bank, Washington D.C.

— 2005. *Doing Business in 2006: Creating Jobs*, World Bank, Washington D.C.

Chapter 7. Process and performance-based regulation: challenges for regulatory governance and regulatory reform

Rex Deighton-Smith

Introduction

Recent decades have seen a substantial move by regulators in Australia, as in many — perhaps most — other OECD countries, toward adopting performance-based and process-based regulation, in preference to traditional prescriptive regulation. Performance based regulation can be defined as regulation that specifies required outputs, rather than inputs and thus provides a degree of freedom to the regulated to determine how they will achieve compliance. Process-based regulation specifies risk identification, assessment and control processes that must be undertaken, documented and (usually) audited. It is most commonly used in contexts in which there are multiple risk sources and multiple feasible risk controls.

This shift in regulatory styles has occurred in pursuit of more effective and efficient regulation and has been almost unanimously welcomed, indeed often vigorously promoted, by regulatory reformers. However, these forms of regulation have many potential drawbacks which have often been insufficiently recognised and inadequately taken into account in regulatory design and implementation. Regulators and regulatory reformers need to act to ensure that the promise of more effective and efficient regulation through the adoption of these newer forms is met in practice. This requires development of a more sophisticated understanding of the nature of these forms of regulation and the critical success factors for their use. Crucially, it requires a more critical approach to the question of whether they are suitable to particular regulatory circumstances: to replace the current tendency to see these regulations as necessarily more 'modern' and superior to prescriptive regulation.

Evidence of the shift

First, it is important to establish the extent of the shift in regulatory styles that has taken place. I will do this by means of a quick tour of the current Australian regulatory landscape. However, as some comparisons made along the way will indicate, in many areas the picture is quite similar in a range of other countries. In sum, it is fair to say that process and performance-based regulation is prominent in all of the major fields in which social regulation exists. That said, it is important to recognise that these three categories of regulation are not mutually exclusive and that many regulatory structures are likely to include elements of two or more regulatory types.

Environmental regulation

Performance based environmental regulation has a history extending over more than two decades. Performance-based 'framework standards' are contained in quasi-regulatory instruments such as 'State Environment Protection Policies'. The works approval process arguably functions as a non-transparent form of process-based regulation. That is, environmental regulators exercise a substantial measure of control over the productive processes that emitters of significant pollutants are able to employ by requiring proposed works that would significantly change existing processes (or implement new ones) to be assessed and approved prior to construction. This process has the objective of enabling a 'whole of process' approach to emissions management to be adopted by effectively requiring company management to take these issues into account in plant and process design. This process-based element is then supplemented by the imposition of specific performance-based emissions standards, tailored to the individual licensee, as part of the licensing process which governs the ongoing operation of the plant.

Rail safety

Rail safety regulation is nationally harmonised and is largely process-based, being built around an accreditation process applicable to all rail operators and infrastructure managers. It requires that a 'safety management system' (SMS) be developed by the operator and assessed and approved by the regulator. The safety management system is based on the identification and assessment of all significant risks and the development of mechanisms by which they are to be controlled. This process is currently being reinforced through the adoption of new national model rail safety legislation, which is expected to specify in substantially greater detail the requirements for SMS and related auditing/approvals arrangements.

Interestingly, this high-level regulatory approach is supplemented in practice by extensive procedures manuals, developed by all significant operators on the basis of the internal regulatory controls that were in use in former times of vertically integrated government-owned rail monopolies. These procedures manuals continue to be largely prescriptive in nature, although they contain some important performance-based elements. For example, one such manual includes a prescriptive requirement that a defined proportion of the brakes on a train must be operational and a performance standard that it must be able to halt within a certain distance.

Food safety

This area is characterised by a mix of all three forms of regulation. A major element of process-based regulation exists, notably through requirements for all 'food premises' to adopt individual Food Safety Programs. At the same time, product standards set out in the Food Standards Code contain an interesting mix of performance-based and prescriptive requirements. For example, the standards relating to cheese contain a prescriptive requirement (milk must be pasteurised before being used for cheese-making), as well as performance-based requirements in the form of maximum allowable bacterial loads.

Occupational health and safety

All Australian OHS acts conform to the 'Robens model', which is based on the specification of the most general of performance standards: the duty to provide a workplace which is safe 'as far as reasonably practicable'. The acts include very broadly specified process-based requirements, for example specifying the 'hierarchy of controls' that must be adopted in undertaking actions to comply with the general duty in different circumstances.

Regulations deal with the interpretation of these duties in a range of specific areas of identified major risk and, in doing so, often adopt a combination of prescriptive requirements and performance standards. For example, Victorian asbestos regulations set out a performance-based exposure standard, which is supplemented by a number of prescriptive requirements, as well as restatements of the general duties applicable and of the required hierarchy of controls to be adopted.

Vehicle design standards

Vehicle standards are internationally harmonised to a large degree — although the USA is a major non-adherent — and based on the United Nations Economic Commission for Europe (UNECE) standards. They are fundamentally performance-based, although they also include significant prescriptive elements in some areas. For example, the door latch regulations are based on a performance standard, requiring that latches be able to withstand a specified pressure but also include a prescriptive requirement that doors must hinge at the front, unless the front door is designed to close over a rear hinged back door.

Building regulation

Technical standards in this area are almost completely nationally harmonised. They are fundamentally performance-based and are supported by 'functional statements' (in common with the vehicle design standards just mentioned) which clearly state the underlying purpose, or objective, of each of the specific regulatory requirements. Building regulation includes, as part of the published regulatory document, a set of 'deemed to satisfy' prescriptive standards aimed at providing certainty of compliance.

This summarises the position in the major areas of social regulation within Australia, in terms of the extent to which process and/or performance-based regulation has been adopted. Of course, the position in Australia is not unique. As I have suggested, there are substantial formal regulatory harmonisation processes in place in some areas, such as vehicle design standards, while in others, such as occupational health and safety, substantially similar regulatory approaches are the results of less formal co-operation between regulators and 'demonstration effects'.

More generally, a number of recent OECD publications have documented the fact that the trend toward increasing use of performance and process-based regulation is visible in the great majority of its member countries. For example, the OECD reported in 2002 that approximately half of member countries stated that they were making increasing use of performance-based regulations in both environmental and health and safety regulation, while a slightly smaller number reported increased use of process-based regulation in these areas (OECD 2002).

Support by regulatory reformers

The advice of regulatory reformers to regulators can generally be summarised as amounting to a fairly uncritical endorsement of the adoption of process and/or performance-based regulation in a wide range of areas. For example, the main guideline document on regulation-making issued by the Council of Australian Governments states:

> … unless prescriptive requirements are unavoidable in order to ensure public safety in high-risk situations, performance-based requirements that specify outcomes rather than inputs or other prescriptive requirements should be used (Council of Australian Governments 2004).

Similarly, the Victorian government's *Guide to Regulation* states that:

> Where appropriate and where permitted by the enabling Act, the Victorian Government encourages the use of performance-based regulation (Victorian Government 2005).

Guidelines as to when performance-based regulation may be appropriate are issued pursuant to the *Subordinate Legislation Act 1994* (Vic). However, apart from making the point that the enabling legislation must permit regulation to be of this type, they say little other than that a benefit/cost approach should be taken and that regulators should be familiar with the characteristics of the regulated industry when making this decision.

The New Zealand regulatory guidance document differs in providing a more balanced view, arguing that:

> Principle and performance-based standards are more appropriate where the outcome can be measured (to ensure compliance) and where innovation is likely to be an important consideration … Prescriptive standards are useful where information costs are high and there is little scope for innovation (New Zealand Government 1999).

Interestingly, neither of the two Australian regulatory guidance documents mentioned above makes any reference at all to process-based regulation, notwithstanding that the quick survey of existing regulatory styles that I have just given suggests that process-based regulation may now be even more widely used than is performance-based regulation. The New Zealand guide refers to 'principle based' regulation, which it defines as regulations that 'describe the objective sought in general terms and require interpretation according to the circumstance' (ibid). Legislation, such as the occupational health and safety (OHS) Acts that specify a range of 'general duties', would fall within this definition.

The relatively uncritical endorsement of these forms of regulation revealed by these quotes reflects a widespread perception among regulatory reform officials that regulators are conservative in their approaches to the use of different policy instruments and largely reliant upon existing approaches. For example, the OECD has written in this context:

> … a crucial challenge for regulatory policies is to encourage cultural changes within regulatory bodies that will ensure that a comparative approach is taken systematically to the question of how best to achieve policy objectives. Efficient and effective policy action is only possible if all available instruments are considered as means of achieving the identified objective. The instruments to be considered include a wide range of non-regulatory instruments, as well as a number of distinctly different forms of regulation (OECD 2002: 52).

If regulators are seen as having strong conservative biases in their choices of policy instrument, it is unsurprising that regulatory reformers would see their main task as being that of promoting relatively new and unfamiliar instruments with the potential for improved efficiency and effectiveness.

The view of regulators as fundamentally conservative and risk adverse in nature is probably fairly soundly based when considering the attitudes of regulators toward replacing regulatory approaches with other, non-regulatory policy instruments, although, even here, it is possible to argue that the propensity of regulators to entertain options such as carbon taxes and emissions trading as responses to global warming is probably greater than that of the politicians that they serve.

However, if there is a degree of risk aversion in relation to non-regulatory policy instruments, the quick tour of current approaches to social regulation I have given casts considerable doubt on the question of whether regulators can truly be said to be averse to adopting regulation that departs from the traditional prescriptive, or 'command and control', form.

If regulators are actually quite open to the use of innovative regulatory instruments, the emphasis of the advice that regulatory reformers are providing to regulators should, arguably, be shifting away from an uncritical promotion of the use of process and performance-based regulation and toward the provision of sophisticated and practical advice regarding both the potential drawbacks of these styles of regulation and the tools that can be used to minimise or avoid these potential problems.

Of course, this proposition rests upon a view that substantial negative impacts can be identified in respect of moves to adopt process and/or performance-based regulation. Consequently, I would now like to identify and analyse some of these potential negative impacts, before moving on to a discussion of how they can be minimised and/or avoided.

Negative impacts and problems — types and evidence

Indiscriminate use

The first of these problems is the increasingly apparent tendency toward the indiscriminate adoption of process or performance-based regulation. Such a tendency is, perhaps unsurprising, given the largely uncritical view of these forms of regulation being promoted in some quarters, including by regulatory reformers, as I have shown.

The adoption of process-based regulation in inappropriate circumstances is particularly problematic. This form of regulation is potentially a powerful tool when the range of risks that need to be controlled is numerous, when some or even many risks may be poorly understood and when a wide range of possible controls exists. In such circumstances, it is nearly impossible to specify an optimal prescriptive approach to regulation and even the use of performance-based regulation may be problematic if appropriate risk standards cannot readily be identified and specified.

However, the adoption of process-based regulation, with its emphasis on management based and systemic controls, is necessarily a relatively 'heavy-handed' approach, in the sense that it inevitably implies quite substantial compliance obligations on affected parties. This suggests that its use should be reserved for situations in which:

- the size of the identified risks that regulation must address is substantial (or the consequences of a single failure are catastrophic, e.g. aviation safety);

- existing regulatory approaches are performing poorly in achieving their underlying objectives, are unduly costly or otherwise subject to a significant measure of 'lack of consent' on the part of the regulated; and
- the regulated industry generally has sufficient capacities to effectively implement the management based requirements of process regulation.

By contrast, where the risks to be mitigated are relatively few and the control measures that can feasibly be employed are also relatively few and well known, there is little likelihood that the specification of a process-based approach will perform better than other alternatives. The application of process-based regulation in these circumstances is likely to lead to strong complaints that the regulatory requirements amount to a costly and time-consuming 'paper chase', with little being achieved as a result.

Some examples of this problem arising from recent Victorian experience are instructive. A requirement, adopted in 2001 in the *Food Act 1984* (Vic), for all food premises to adopt a Food Safety Plan effectively applied process regulation to all corner cafes and the like. This implied a massive paperwork burden in a context in which risks were few and well defined, as were the appropriate controls. Small businesses saw the requirement to develop the plans as a massive compliance burden, given their unfamiliarity with the processes required, as well as leading to a situation in which they had no certainty that their resulting plan would be found to be compliant. The resulting outcry effectively forced the government to develop and propagate 'template' food safety plans to act as guidance for such businesses.

In practice, it seems that little customisation of these templates occurred. The fact that template food safety programs *could* be developed effectively constitutes an admission of the inappropriateness of applying process-based regulation in this context, as it showed that broadly applicable risk controls could be identified and specified in a quasi-regulatory document. However, this did not prevent the proposal of similar requirements for all dentists across Victoria, covering the use of x-ray machines. These requirements would have been implemented under the *Radiation Act 2007* (Vic). Here again, small dental practices would be required to undertake the whole risk identification, assessment and control process when, in fact, the requirements of their registration as dentists already included elements of regulation of the use of x-ray machines.

In the event, recently implemented requirements for regulatory impact assessment to be conducted on draft legislation identified the disproportionate costs involved and convinced the regulators to drop the proposal. However, without such controls, it is highly likely that the developing 'orthodoxy' among regulators in favour of process-based regulation would have led to its use in this obviously inappropriate context.

These are examples of areas in which the basic rationale for process-based regulation, that is, that there are multiple sources of risk and multiple potential means of addressing those risks, are not met. However, in some other circumstances in which these 'threshold' conditions are met, substantial problems have still arisen due to the process-based regulatory requirements being applied across too broad a scope.

The food safety case I have just cited is also an example of this dynamic. Another example is the recent adoption of new rail safety legislation in Victoria. While rail operations clearly do constitute an appropriate context in which to implement process-based regulation, the scope of the legislation and specifically its requirements for accreditation and the preparation of detailed Safety Management Systems, was broadened to the point where tourism and heritage sector operators were also required to conform to these requirements. Thus, organisations running very small scale rail operations and relying largely or wholly on volunteer labour are being asked to undertake the whole risk identification and assessment process, document the findings, submit them for regulatory approval and have them audited on a regular basis. While there was some debate as to whether these operators might be excluded, it appears that the decision to expand the scope of process-based regulation to include this group was essentially a political one.

In the event, the political solution to the problem generated by the poor decision on regulatory scope is that government will subsidise the sector to complete the regulatory obligations that have been imposed upon it. This surely constitutes recognition that the public would not willingly accept that the necessary consequence of expanding the regulatory reach of the new requirements into these areas would otherwise be the closure of substantial parts of the tourism and heritage rail sector.

Negative combinations of process, performance & prescriptive regulations

A second set of problems relates to the frequent failure of regulators to produce logical, mutually supportive combinations of process, performance and/or prescriptive regulation. Certainly, many or even most regulatory structures need to combine at least two of these types of regulation in order to achieve an efficient and effective whole. However, there seems to be little understanding of how these combinations ought to be achieved. Again, a couple of examples can highlight the problem.

The first relates to the *Australia New Zealand Food Standards Code* and specifically the part of it that deals with cheese-making. This part constitutes a wholly dysfunctional combination of prescriptive and performance-based regulation, as was made apparent in an Administrative Appeals Tribunal hearing in 2003.[1] The prescriptive requirement is that milk used to make cheese must be pasteurised. The performance standard specifies the maximum allowable bacterial load. As cheese is defined as a high-risk product, a certain proportion of cheeses must be tested on importation and the bacterial load shown to be below the performance standard. The AAT hearing arose because an importer of cheese made from unpasteurised milk wished to have it tested and approved for sale on the basis that it met the performance standard. AQIS argued that it was not required to test the cheese until he could show that the cheese had met the prescriptive standard. The AAT upheld the AQIS viewpoint, based on its reading of the letter of the code, notwithstanding that AQIS did not make any claim that the cheese in question was unsafe for human consumption. Despite this demonstrated absurdity, the code has not been amended and the cheese in question is on sale now in Australia only because it went through an expensive and time consuming 'exemption' process which must audit the entire cheese-making process in order to prove that it will systematically lead to the production of 'safe' cheese.

A second type of dysfunctional combination of performance and prescriptive standards relates to the widespread use of Deemed to Satisfy (DTS) standards. These are generally prescriptive standards drafted in order to provide guidance on means of compliance, particularly for small business and therefore to improve the certainty of compliance with performance-based regulation. Their use, in many circumstances, is an almost inevitable adjunct to the adoption of performance-based regulation.

However, two problems can be identified. First, most of Australia's occupational health and safety legislation arguably makes this material 'quasi-compulsory' by reversing the onus of proof, such that employers who do not use the DTS material must, in the event of a prosecution, prove that they achieved 'an equivalent level of safety'[2] by alternative means. Thus, the performance-based legislation is effectively supplemented by a substantial body of detailed, prescriptive quasi-legislation.

Second, even where this issue of a reversal of the onus of proof is not relevant, the adoption of large quantities of DTS material will still tend, in many circumstances, to lead to a 'reading up' of the compliance obligations established in the performance-based regulation. This problem may be exacerbated by the fact that there is often relatively little attention paid to the drafting quality of the DTS material, as it is seen as having guidance status rather than constituting regulation. Thus, while a high proportion of businesses may use the DTS material as the basis for their regulatory compliance efforts, it's technical quality may be substantially less than that of the prescriptive regulation that it has, in many cases, replaced. This is particularly the case where large numbers of technical standards are adopted in the DTS material, as this kind of material is not generally drafted with legislative compliance issues in mind.

To take just one example, a quick search of the NSW *Occupational Health and Safety Regulation 2001* reveals that it calls up 30 Australian Standards and five National Occupational Health and Safety Commission standards. This demonstrates a third area of concern: while performance-based regulation has often been promoted, in part, because it supposedly simplifies regulatory requirements (by replacing detailed prescriptive requirements with simple outcome standards) the result is very often the reverse. The total volume of the technical standards one must read and digest in order to reach a clear understanding of the regulatory meaning may be many times larger than the previous body of prescriptive regulation.

Thus, while the supplementation of performance-based standards with DTS material is probably virtually inevitable, in most regulatory contexts, there is a strong danger that excessive use of this mechanism will effectively contribute to significant increases in regulatory complexity and cost, particularly because of the relative absence of regulatory quality controls on such 'grey letter' law.

I should note that this issue of the overuse of technical standards has been recognised for some years now, with some regulatory guidance material advising a sceptical approach (or at least a careful one) should be taken to their adoption in regulation. However, as a recent Productivity Commission report suggests, with around 2300 Australian Standards (one third of the total) alone now being incorporated 'by reference' in Australian law, there seems to have been little progress made (Productivity Commission 2006: xiv).

Lack of clearly defined compliance requirements

Process and performance-based legislation also often suffers from an absence of clearly identified standards as to compliance obligations. This issue was highlighted in the recent *Maxwell Report*, which reviewed the Victorian occupational health and safety legislation that had been in place since the mid-1980s (Maxwell 2004). Maxwell made recommendations intended to deal with this issue. However, their implementation by government appears to have had a perverse outcome.

The core issue is that the general duty on employers has historically been to provide 'as far as is reasonably practicable' a safe workplace. This is an example of what in New Zealand is referred to as 'principles based' regulation. Maxwell recommended that the legislation should explicitly state that this standard involves a requirement to take action to reduce risk up to the point at which the costs of the risk reduction activity became 'grossly disproportionate' to the benefit obtained from the risk reduction (Maxwell 2004: 125-34).

This test is itself clearly open to some interpretation. However, Maxwell explicitly contrasted this test with the benefit/cost framework that is statutorily required to be used in Regulatory Impact Assessment (RIA) and which, for an economist is consistent with societal welfare maximisation. Maxwell makes clear that the 'gross disproportion' test would require that actions be taken with costs that significantly exceed benefits in many cases. However, he fails to discuss or resolve the conflict inherent in his proposing primary legislation that sets an entirely different test of employer duties from that to which any subordinate legislation made under its authority must be subjected.

Interestingly, it has not taken long for other regulators to recognise this problem. This has led to be adoption in the new *Rail Safety Act 2006* (Vic) of an alternative form of words: the duty of rail organisations is to control risk 'So Far As Is Reasonably Practicable'. According to the regulators involved, it was intended that the 'gross disproportion' test would not apply, as it was considered impractical and unduly onerous to apply this standard to the industry.

However, while this is the intent behind establishing alternative wording for the relevant test, it remains far from clear that it has been achieved and will presumably await the development of case law for this question to be determined.

RIA problems

A very significant problem with performance-based and, especially, process-based legislation is that it can become almost impossible to undertake reasonable *ex ante* RIA on regulation that is framed in these terms. In particular, there is little prospect of developing robust *ex ante* analyses of requirements to develop SMS and to develop risk controls based upon those SMS. This problem is particularly acute when legislation gives little explicit detail as to the required content of SMS and relies overly on the discretion of regulators in this regard. In this context, there must be substantial uncertainty as to whether regulation of this sort will produce net benefits for society, while the legitimacy of the RIA process is also undermined as a result.

This problem is compounded by the fact that the spur for the adoption of process-based regulation in a particular circumstance is often not any clearly identified and measured problems with the outcomes achieved under existing regulation but, rather, a desire to adopt 'best practice' regulation — with process-based regulation increasingly being seen in this light regardless of the specific regulatory circumstance. Thus — and I say this from the viewpoint of a consultant who undertakes a great deal of RIA — there can be major challenges at both the 'problem identification' stage and in terms of developing the argument that process-based regulation is likely to lead to superior regulatory performance than existing arrangements: there is often no identifiable regulatory failure when outcomes are considered, yet very substantial new compliance obligations are being proposed. As an example, new rail safety legislation in Victoria has been estimated to impose over $20 million in additional regulatory costs over 10 years and is being imposed in a context in which the incidence of rail fatalities has shown a continuing declining trend over more than two decades and, considered in an international context, is already running at levels well below OECD averages.

Equity and accountability issues

Process-based regulation, in particular, often lacks legitimacy with the public and, in some cases, with regulated entities owing to concerns that it does not necessarily ensure equal, or equitable, treatment for different regulated entities. This concern arises from the degree of discretion, or judgment required to be exercised by the regulatory agency in assessing compliance with, for example, an SMS requirement. Arguably, this issue largely constitutes a specific case of the general issue of regulatory transparency: that is, that many of these concerns can be addressed by regulators being more open about the criteria used for judgment, such as by publishing guidance material on relevant issues.

Finally, a long-standing concern with the use of performance standards, which is also relevant to process-based regulation, relates to the availability of various 'incorporated texts'. As I have already suggested, performance-based regulation often leans heavily on supplementary material that is prescriptive in nature and which often has deemed-to-comply status but may also be compulsory. The use of Australian Standards in this context is particularly widespread. The key issue here is that these standards must be purchased at substantial cost and frequently updated. By contrast, legislation has traditionally been published at minimal cost, while there is an increasing expectation that legislation will be available online at no charge.

Some possible solutions

In raising all of these problems and concerns, I certainly do not mean to suggest that the use of either process-based or performance-based regulation is, on balance, a negative for regulatory quality. Rather, I want to highlight the need for a better understanding of the nature of these regulatory tools and, in particular, of the specific regulatory contexts in which their use is being considered. Also needed is more careful regulatory design and development that takes account of this context. The following highlights major issues in ensuring this is achieved.

Ensure adequate understanding of the regulatory context

This implies one must:

- understand the nature of the risks being regulated and the possible solutions before determining what form of regulation is preferred;
- only use process-based approaches where there are multiple risk sources and multiple possible risk controls; and

- only use performance-based regulation when it is possible to specify clearly the required outcome standards and, again, where there are likely to be different ways of achieving them and/or innovation is likely to be an important factor.

Understand the regulated industry

When considering process or performance-based regulation, consider the capacities of regulated parties: will it be feasible and proportionate to ask them to undertake the required compliance processes?

If process-based regulation appears appropriate, consider how small business compliance issues will be dealt with.

Appropriate use of DTS material

When developing DTS standards, consider the overall volume of regulatory and quasi-regulatory material and assess this against the question of feasibility of regulatory compliance.

In this context, remember that regulation should set a framework for compliance efforts, not attempt to set out a prescriptive requirement for all conceivable circumstances.

When adopting existing materials as DTS standards, consider whether they are drafted in ways that are appropriate for interpretation in a regulatory context. If not, consider the need to draft new materials specifically for this purpose.

Combining regulatory forms

Consider the relationships between prescriptive, performance and/or process-based regulatory elements, ensuring that they are mutually supportive rather than antagonistic. For example, setting out prescriptive regulatory requirements but providing for exemptions to be provided where process-based alternative approaches are adopted is likely to be an effective combination. Setting out both a prescriptive and a performance-based standard and requiring both to be met (rather than either) is not likely to be effective.

Role of regulatory policy/regulatory reform bodies

Responsibility for making more sophisticated and effective choices among regulatory alternatives obviously rests primarily with regulators. However, regulatory reformers have a potentially major role to play — these issues are at the core of what the OECD calls 'regulatory policy'.

As a first step, regulatory policy must abandon the almost uncritical promotion of these forms of regulation in favour of a more sophisticated message. A major element of this would be developing more sophisticated regulatory guidance material that looks at issues of linking regulatory context and regulatory design and goes into some detail on aspects of regulatory design.

Enhanced controls as part of regulatory policy

The provision of improved advice and guidance on the use regulation should also be accompanied by the adoption of a 'challenge' function as one of the responsibilities of regulatory reform authorities. This challenge model already exists in some jurisdictions including, to a degree, the Australian Federal government. The issue here is necessarily broader than the question of the use of performance or process-based regulation. However, providing regulatory reform authorities with the power, or responsibility, to act positively to challenge what they believe to be poor regulatory practices could be particularly important improving the way that these forms of regulation are being used.

Finally, I suspect that this is an area in which regulatory reform authorities may themselves frequently have limited expertise and understanding. This suggests the need for significant development activity, both through research of the relevant literature and, potentially, through working cooperatively with regulators in the development and implementation of practical models combining different regulatory types.

References

Council of Australian Governments 2004, 'Principles and Guidelines for National Standard Setting and Regulatory Action by Ministerial Councils and Standard-Setting Bodies', viewed at 11 October 2007, http://coag.gov.au/meetings/250604/coagpg04.pdf

Department of Treasury and Finance 2005, 'Rewards from Reform: Higher Productivity and Labour Participation', August.

Department of Treasury and Finance 2006, 'Reducing the Regulatory Burden: The Victorian Government's Plan to reduce red tape'.

International Monetary Fund 2006, *Public Information Notice (PIN) No. 06/123*, page 3, October 23, at http://www.imf.org/external/pubs/ft/scr/2006/cr06374.pdf

Maxwell, C. 2004, *Occupational Health and Safety Act Review*, State of Victoria, March 2004.

New Zealand Government 1999, *A Guide to Preparing Regulatory Impact Statements*, Ministry of Commerce.

OECD 2002, 'Regulatory Policies in OECD Countries: From Interventionism to Regulatory Governance', OECD, Paris.

Productivity Commission 2006, 'Standard Setting and Laboratory Accreditation'. Draft Research Report, Productivity Commission.

ENDNOTES

[1] Studd vs Secretary to the Department of Agriculture, Fisheries and Forestry (AATA897, 12 September 2003).

[2] This term was used in S56 of the former Victorian *Occupational Health and Safety Act* 1985. Similar provisions allowing non-compliance with a Code to be admitted in evidence in OHS prosecutions exist in, for example, S42 of the Queensland legislation and S46 of the NSW legislation.

Chapter 8. Conclusion

Peter Carroll

As noted, the bulk of the chapters in this book other than the introduction and this conclusion were presented originally as separate conference papers on a related theme. Hence, while each of the papers addresses an aspect of the second or third waves of regulatory reform that have taken place in Australia since the mid-1980s, focused on reforms to processes, they were not designed to fit together in a coherent whole as chapters in a book. Moreover, the papers were presented before COAG had reached any final agreement on the National Reform Agenda (NRA) — the third wave of reform. Nevertheless, as we hope the reader will agree, they do provide a valuable set of perspectives about the various processes of regulatory reform as a whole, as well as important, specific issues that have arisen. In this context three broad conclusions reached in the chapters are identified and, as far as possible, related to the final COAG agreement on the NRA.

The first is that while the reforms have improved the quality of the processes associated with the making of regulation, the level of improvement has been variable in both extent and impact. The second is that reform should continue, as has been agreed by COAG, in terms of both building on the established achievements as well as remedying the reforms that have been less successful. The third is that the primary focus of regulatory reform in Australia, at least at the federal level, has focused on regulatory simplification and efficiency, rather neglecting the issue of how to manage regulatory complexity.

With regard to the first conclusion, the main vehicle of process reform has been the RIS system, though with variable results. Perhaps the fundamental and inevitable difficulty its proponents face is that policy-making is an inherently political process — one that is embedded in a liberal-democratic system of government. This is a difficulty — perhaps an insurmountable one — as the wishes of the electorate do not always coincide with the requirements of a rational decision-making process such as that at the core of the RIS process. Rather, politics involves constantly changing activities and processes arising from the interaction of individual and group values, motivations and actions, notably in situations of scarce human and physical resources. Both conflict and cooperation can result and, while conflict is not an inevitable result of such interactions, it is a very frequent characteristic, especially where individuals and groups compete, successfully and unsuccessfully, for the scarce resources they see as necessary to achieve their goals or where they compete in relation to values (or both). It often requires a series of compromises between the competing parties before agreement can be reached as to the content of a new or modified regulation.

When the set of compromises that constitute a regulation are subject to rational analysis in terms of the more rigorous criteria utilised in a cost-benefit analysis, they are likely to 'fail' to meet the criteria or tests mandated under RIS. But RIS does not test for the merits of the compromises underlying the regulation. It is silent as to whether a regulation meets the criteria for political success. Hence, it is not surprising that ministers, their minders and senior public servants have reservations about the value of RIS, reservations that are visible in their varying degrees of commitment to the process. However, it is important that all of these actors, as well as the constituencies they represent, are made aware of the costs and the benefits of the compromises they have reached. In a very real sense, a good RIS — one that includes a rigorous financial analysis or cost-benefit analysis — indicates the cost of politics for a democratic system: costs that should always be born in mind by decision-makers.

While not explicit, elements of the above view about the constraints imposed upon rational decision-making by the political system are contained within COAG's 2007 Communiqué regarding the NRA (COAG 2007). This is most obvious in relation to two areas: one, the requirement for a new system of annual reviews where each government conducts annual, targeted reviews; and two, an agreement for an intergovernmental, benchmarking study of the compliance costs of regulation (COAG 2007: 9-10).

The annual reviews of selected regulation are to involve a public inquiry and reporting process that provides opportunities for input from a range of stakeholders, with the review recommendations to be acted upon by each government (COAG 2007: 9). While this will not avoid the inevitable politics associated with the making of regulation, it will, if successful, help ensure that the compromises, costs and benefits of significant regulatory decisions as embodied in the selected regulation, will be reviewed in a public context and on a regular basis. The result, hopefully, will be regulatory compromises that impose least costs on the community, if not perfectly rational regulation.

The benchmarking proposal will have a salutary impact on the politics of regulation as it will make public the relative costs of the compromises embodied in comparable regulation in each of the member governments, notably the state governments. In particular, the comparative costs to business of complying with regulation will be made available. While the impact of such knowledge is uncertain, it is not difficult to imagine a number of scenarios. One might be the 'regulatory competition' scenario. In this scenario 'benchmarking data' will lead to a demand from business for new or modified regulations that impose either no greater cost, or less cost, than the comparable regulations in the other jurisdictions, as shown by the bench mark studies. While the specifics of business demands will vary, firms and their industry associations will tend to put forward the argument that they are, or will be disadvantaged by competition from products or services produced in the other jurisdictions where the cost of regulation is less.

If we assume that the demands of business for the lower cost regulation are accepted, then the governments involved have a number of options. At the simplest level this might involve little more than a simple copying of regulation from the 'least cost' state, perhaps for a decrease in the fees charged to business. However, at times more substantial policy innovation will be necessary in designing new and less cost regulation, imposing greater workloads on the policy developers involved. If local policy design capacity is limited, or an existing regulatory design seems most efficient, then there is likely to be an increase in the policy transfer of less costly regulation from the states with less costly regulatory regimes to the states with more costly regimes. Policy innovation by means of policy transfer — or copying from other states — is already commonplace, but benchmarking may increase its frequency, given the need for rapid policy responses in a competitive regulatory environment. It might also lead to a greater role for COAG in determining whether or not a regulation should be harmonised across all member governments.

Indeed, there are dangers in this regard as the costs of developing the necessary innovative regulatory capacity might be seen as too great at the state government level, leading to a tendency to encourage and support a system for harmonising regulation that draws less heavily upon their limited resources. This might be an appropriate response where the regulation that is harmonised is the most effective, least-cost option. However, those who support the value of competitive markets would point out that a system of 'managed' harmonised regulation that lacks the stimulus of competition is not likely to be the most efficient or effective. Rather, it would tend to exhibit the costly features of a cartel-type arrangement.

A final decision on the benchmarking exercise will not be made by COAG until after the results of the Productivity Commission studies are known. However, assuming that the results are convincing, the benchmarking of the regulatory costs of similar regulation in place in each jurisdiction might stimulate the production of more effective and efficient regulation — provided that it does not lead to the cartel-like situation noted above.

The second conclusion — that reforms to regulatory processes and associated techniques should continue, building on its successes, as well as remedying its failures — is one that was endorsed by COAG in the context of the National Reform Agenda (NRA). It is evident, for example, in the agreements for annual reviews and regulatory benchmarking. In addition, it can be seen in the agreements that all members would:

... establish and maintain effective arrangements at each level of government that maximise the efficiency of new and amended regulation and avoid unnecessary compliance costs and restrictions on competition by:

(a) establishing and maintaining 'gate keeping mechanisms' as part of the decision-making process to ensure that the regulatory impact of proposed regulatory instruments are made fully transparent to decision-makers in advance of decisions being made and to the public as soon as possible;

(b) improving the quality of regulation impact analysis through the use, where appropriate, of cost-benefit analysis; better measurement of compliance costs flowing from new and amended regulation, such as through the use of the Commonwealth Office of Small Business' costing model;

(c) broadening the scope of regulation impact analysis, where appropriate, to recognise the effect of regulation on individuals and the cumulative burden on business and, as part of the consideration of alternatives to new regulation, have regard to whether the existing regulatory regimes of other jurisdictions might offer a viable alternative; and

(d) applying these arrangements to Ministerial Councils (COAG 2007).

While the specific means by which each jurisdiction is to achieve the above aims is not specified, each member has provided a progress report against an 'Intergovernmental Action Plan', on the actions it has taken — or plans to take — to implement the aims (COAG 2006; and 2007: 15-22). Their reports indicate substantial variation in their interpretation of the meaning of the agreements as well as some variation in their progress in implementation. With regard to the latter, most governments indicated that the agreed changes to process and techniques have, or would be put in place in 2007, with the exception of Tasmania (which provided no indication of expected completion dates).

With regard to variations in interpretation, the Commonwealth government, for example, has adopted a very 'hard line' as regards the adoption of gate-keeping mechanisms by requiring that its Cabinet Secretariat not circulate final submissions or memoranda to cabinet members without an adequate RIS or compliance cost assessment other than in 'exceptional circumstances' (COAG 2007: 15). Judgements about the adequacy of RISs are to be made by the Productivity Commission's Office of Best Practice Regulation. In contrast, the NSW Government, in relation to gate-keeping requirements, will require an assessment of adequacy by a new Better Regulation Office and a certification of adequacy by a minister with specific responsibility for regulatory reform (COAG 2007:17-18). It makes no mention as to whether or not regulatory proposals that are judged 'not adequate' or 'not certified' will be submitted to cabinet for consideration. In further contrast, the WA Government's report notes only that 'enhanced gate keeping arrangements' will be put in place, without indicating what will be the case if submissions are not adequate or complete (COAG 2007: 21). The key question to be asked is whether or not the combination of progress reports and peer pressure will result in significant progress in the improvement of regulatory processes in all jurisdictions. This is a question that cannot be answered, in all fairness, until more time has elapsed.

The third conclusion, that the capacity of Australian governments to manage regulatory complexity needs to be improved, has not been directly addressed by COAG in the NRA. Rather, its general goal with regard to regulation is to reduce what is seen as the regulatory burden on business imposed by the three levels of government (COAG 2006). It could be argued (although COAG's reports do not do so) that: one, the NRA's general goal of improving regulatory performance does include an implied commitment to improving the governments' capacity to manage regulatory complexity, a complexity that will continue even where the regulatory burden is reduced and simplified; two, that this is the primary responsibility of the Australian Public Service Commission (APSC). However, a detailed examination of the COAG agreements reveals no recognition of the need to improve the management of regulatory complexity, nor any reference to any related role of the APSC in pursuing such improvements. Instead, there is only a continuing emphasis on regulation-making and review, but not day to day management. Similarly, a perusal of two recent, major APSC documents, the 'Building Better Governance', guidelines, and the 'Tackling Wicked Problems' report, both released in 2007, make no reference to the National Reform Agenda, the role of COAG in that regard, or how the guidelines might support the achievement of the improved management of regulatory complexity (APSC 2007a: 2007b).

In 2007 a new Australian Labor Party government under Prime Minister Kevin Rudd came into office. It is committed to a continuing program of regulatory reform, including those put forward by the Taskforce on Regulation in 2006, arguing that the Howard governments had failed to continue the microeconomic reform process instigated by Labor governments in the 1980s and 1990s, with the result that the regulatory burden had grown and Australian productivity had fallen (Emerson 2007). In relation to regulatory processes three significant changes were introduced by the new Government in late 2007 that signified its reform commitments: one, the renaming of the existing core Department of Finance and Administration as the Department of Finance and Deregulation (DFD); two, the transfer of responsibility for regulatory reform from Treasury to the DFD; three, the relocation of the Office of Best Practice Regulation (OBPR) from the Productivity Commission to DFD, within its Financial Management Division, with a new Minister Assisting the Finance Minister on Deregulation,

Dr Craig Emerson. In essence, the three changes constituted a centralisation within one organisational location of the previously separate areas largely responsible for regulatory reform in the Commonwealth administration. Moreover, the DFD, with its long tradition of rigorous assessment of the budgets and financial management practices of the line departments, was in a position to add both experience and increased competence to the scrutiny of departmental RIAs. The decision to use the term 'deregulation', in the department's title is significant, implying a commitment to cut what many see as the increasing regulatory burden on business, not merely to engage in regulatory reform. It sends a clear and very sympathetic signal to the peak business associations and the Productivity Commission that had been arguing for more effort in this regard, although the extent to which deregulation actually occurs remains to be seen.

In conclusion, the last three decades have seen repeated attempts to improve Australia's regulatory processes and systems based on the assumption that better regulatory outputs and outcomes can best be achieved by improving the capacity and design of the systems for making and modifying regulation. Those attempts have had varying degrees of success and, while the most recent, third wave of reform is the most ambitious in its scope, committing all COAG members to a wide range of activities aimed at further improvement, its outcome is likely, again, to be variable, although the new Rudd government is clearly committed to those reforms.

References

APSC 2007a, *Building Better Governance*, viewed on 12 November 2007, at http://www.apsc.gov.au/publications07/bettergovernance.pdf

APSC 2007, *Tackling Wicked Problems*, viewed on 12 November 2007, at http://www.apsc.gov.au/publications07/wickedproblems.pdf

Australian Government 2006a, *Rethinking Regulation: Report of the Taskforce on Reducing Regulatory Burdens on Business Interim Response*, as at 28 June 2006, at http://www.pm.gov.au/news/media_releases/media_Release1869.html

Australian Government 2006b, 'Rethinking Regulation: Report of the Taskforce on Reducing Regulatory Burdens on Business Australian Government's Response'.

COAG 2004, 'Principles and Guidelines for National Standard Setting and Regulatory Action by Ministerial Councils and Standard-Setting Bodies', viewed on 12 November 2007 at http://www.obpr.gov.au/_data/assets/pdf_file/0011/69662/coag.pdf

— 2006, *Council of Australian Governments' Meeting 10 February 2006*, viewed on 12 November 2007, at http://coag.gov.au/meetings/100206/index.htm#reform

— 2007, *COAG Regulatory Reform Plan*, viewed on 12 November 2007, at http://coag.gov.au/meetings/130407/docs/coag_nra_regulatory_reform.pdf

Emerson, C, 2007. 'Lifting productivity growth by reducing business regulation', as at the Australian Labor Party website at 9 January 2008, at http://www.alp.org.au/download/now/lifting_productivity_growth_by_reducing_business_regulation_22apr07.pdf